AN
ESSENTIAL
UNITY

A Contemporary Look at Lutheran and Episcopal Liturgies

David L. Veal

MOREHOUSE PUBLISHING
HARRISBURG, PENNSYLVANIA

Copyright © 1997 by David L. Veal

Morehouse Publishing

Editorial Office:
871 Ethan Allen Hwy.
Ridgefield, CT 06877

Corporate Office:
P.O. Box 1321
Harrisburg, PA 17105

Library of Congress Cataloging-in-Publication Data
Veal, David, 1938-
    An essential unity : a contemporary look at Lutheran and Episcopal liturgies / David Veal.
      p. cm.
    ISBN 0-8192-1698-4 (pbk.)
    1. Episcopal Church. Book of common prayer (1979) 2. Lutheran book of worship. 3. Lord's Supper (Liturgy)—comparative studies. 4. Baptism (Liturgy)—Comparative studies. 5. Episcopal Church—Relations—Lutheran Church. 6. Lutheran Church—Relations—Episcopal Church. 7. Christian union conversations—United States.
    I. Title
    BX5946.V43   1997   97-12056
    264'.03—dc21   CIP

Printed in the United States of America

CONTENTS

FOREWORD

This book is for Lutherans and Episcopalians, laity and clergy. It is our hope that it will not appear pedantic or so erudite or pretentious as to turn off an interested lay person. Yet, it is also our hope that it will not be so elementary as to bore the reader who has the benefit of a theological education. We would be delighted if it should prove interesting to some of our other ecumenical partners in Christ's flock: Methodists, Presbyterians, Disciples, Roman Catholics, Eastern Orthodox, and others. Our most precious hope is that in holding up these two great liturgies that have so much in common we might be lifting up an icon to serve as a vehicle of praise to God and encouragement to all Christians that we can find peace and unity among ourselves and with God in "true worship" which, after all, is what *orthodoxy* really is.

The Reverend Canon David L. Veal
The Nativity of Saint John the Baptist, 1996

PREFACE

As we Episcopalians and Lutherans strive to live into our Agreement of 1982 through mutual prayer and support; common study of the Holy Scriptures, histories and theological traditions of each church, and material from the dialogues; joint programs of religious education, theological discussion, mission, evangelism, and social action; joint use of facilities; and through interim sharing of the eucharist, we need resources to help us accomplish such common life and mission. This need will be intensified if the proposed Concordat of Agreement is voted into reality in 1997.

This book will be invaluable for laity and clergy alike as we try to learn about, understand, and appreciate one another. Canon Veal offers a side-by-side comparison of the eucharistic and baptismal liturgies from the 1979 *Book of Common Prayer* and the *Lutheran Book of Worship*, with facing commentaries pointing to similarities and commonalties. There are any number of fascinating liturgical and historical insights as well, to help us appreciate how strong our common roots are.

An Essential Unity could be used in a variety of situations: for personal study; for joint study before a shared eucharist or baptism; as a resource for preparing instructed eucharists and baptisms; as a guide for study of our liturgical traditions and their roots; for seminarians; for clergy study programs. Indeed, I learned a great deal about Episcopal liturgy, and I am a cradle Episcopalian!

Canon Veal is to be commended for preparing this resource to help us live into the Lutheran-Episcopal Agreement of 1982 and to prepare for the day when our churches will enter into full communion with one another.

MIDGE ROOF, President
Episcopal Diocesan Ecumenical Officers

LUTHERANS, EPISCOPALIANS, AND LITURGY

We are "good protestant catholics." So wrote Captain John Smith of his little band of settlers in Jamestown, Virginia. The meaning of his terminology was clear in 1607. Later, English-speaking America was powerfully influenced by radical Calvinists and still later by Roman Catholics. A severe polarization resulted so that "Protestant" and "Catholic" became antonyms. Indeed, they came to be seen as names of two different religions! Most people in the sixteenth century Church of England saw themselves and their branch of the church universal as loyal to the fundamentals of the catholic, orthodox, and apostolic faith, and "Protestant" in the sense that they rejected the abuses, innovations, and distortions of the medieval and renaissance Roman Church of Western Europe.

In much the same way, the Evangelical Christians who came to be called "Lutherans" did not think of themselves as abandoning the historical church or the catholic, orthodox, and apostolic faith and practice. On the contrary, they felt that they were restoring, continuing, and renewing truly catholic ways. "Our churches teach that one holy church is to continue forever," reads Article VII of the Augsburg Confession. And further, when they wrote, "Inasmuch as our churches dissent from the church catholic in no article of faith but only omit some few abuses which are new and have been adopted by the faults of the times" the Lutherans of the Reformation era made it clear that they did not intend to depart from catholic faith and practice.

During the Reformation both Lutherans and Anglicans

(Episcopalians) turned to the gospel of Jesus Christ and to the faith and practices that the incarnate Lord and the apostles clearly instituted. In Jesus Christ and the gospel they saw the essence of the true catholic teaching of the church. They translated the Scriptures and proclaimed the gospel in the churches in languages the people could understand. Their work of translation and reform of the church's liturgy, her public worship, were at the very heart of what they were striving mightily to do: to make the *Evangel*, the good news of God in Christ, available and accessible to the people.

Both churches are liturgical. Both maintain prescribed and carefully governed guidelines, texts, and directions for the conduct of public worship. For the people of God well-ordered liturgy is one of the best protections against eccentric, fanatic, or poorly educated clergy. It helps guard against heresy and assures a reasonable measure of orthodoxy in teaching and practice. A good, fixed liturgy enables the people to participate in the worship of God to the fullest extent. The church's liturgy guarantees variety and the presentation of all the fundamental gospel themes through the course of the year. The basic structure of the traditional Christian liturgy is catholic and apostolic. That is, the liturgy that is used by both Lutherans and Episcopalians is a continuing expression of "the faith once for all delivered to the saints." It is, in its essentials, not limited to one particular culture or time but is "for all people in all times and in all places." It is not sectarian, but is a part of the heritage of the whole church catholic. It is inherited from apostolic times and has been passed on to us through centuries of use, interpretation, and translation. It is a part of the lore of the community that was "sent" (Greek, *apostolos*) into human history by Christ and the apostles and has been received and passed on, enriched by generation after generation of Christian people. This liturgy is a part of what Anglicans sometimes call Tradition, with a capital T. To them it is authoritative in the sense that it is a very important vehicle through which the faith and practice of Christ and the apostles are preserved and communicated. Tradition is one leg of the proverbial "three-legged stool" of Anglicanism: Scripture, Tradition, Reason. For Lutherans it is probably not quite so authoritative, but Lutherans also have a profound respect for the apostolic Tradition and no intention of abandoning the fundamental liturgical practices of the universal church. The liturgy is the principal vessel in which the "Word and Sacrament" are carried. Both Lutheran and Anglican doctrinal formulas define the church as existing where the Word is proclaimed and the Sacraments observed.

Liturgy is what we call corporate prayer and worship, as distinguished from private or individual prayer and worship. Liturgy is, literally, "the work of the people" (Greek, *leitourgia*). One of the principal goals of the Reformation of the sixteenth century in both Germany and England was to enable the people to participate more fully in public worship. The Roman Catholic Council, Vatican II, in 1963 proclaimed that the church "earnestly desires that all the faithful should be led to that full, conscious, and active participation in liturgical celebrations which is demanded by the very nature of the liturgy" (from the *Constitution on the Sacred Liturgy*, paragraph 14). Unless we do it together, it is not liturgy. A solo or a speech may be deeply religious and inspiring, but it is not liturgy. When dancers perform before a congregation, that is not liturgical dance. When a whole congregation of Shakers or Ethiopians dance together in praise of God, that is liturgical dance.

A significant degree of familiarity and prior agreement is necessary for liturgy to happen. An individual may make up his own song as he goes along, but a chorus or a congregation must decide ahead of time about what they are going to sing and they have to be familiar with the same words and music. It is common familiarity with the words and music that enables a group of evangelicals to sing "Amazing Grace" together with meaning and with feeling. It is common familiarity with the words and music that enables a group of Christians to pray and worship together with meaning and sincerity.

Episcopalians have always taken very seriously the liturgy of the church, which they call the "common prayer." They have tended to be more rigid than Lutherans and to be more insistent on conformity when it comes to corporate worship. This inclination stems from a strong Anglican commitment to the principle of *lex orandi lex credendi* (Latin, "the law of praying is the law of believing") which means that they pray their faith and seek to live together as they pray together. The modern Church of England was profoundly shaped by the Elizabethan Settlement of the sixteenth century, and the cornerstone of that Settlement was not its confessional statements or its ecclesiastical structure but, rather, its Book of Common Prayer. In the public services of the church, carefully prescribed by the Book of Common Prayer, there was an integration and presentation of Bible and sacraments, creed and ministry; of the doctrine, discipline, and worship of the church. This has been no less true of Episcopalians in America. To this day the Constitution of the Episcopal Church in this country clearly states: "The Book of Common Prayer, as now established or hereafter amended by the authority of this Church, shall be in use in all the Dioceses of this Church." The canons of the Episcopal Church are quite specific about the offenses for which bishops, priests, or deacons may be presented and tried. Those offenses include any "violation of the rubrics of the Book of Common Prayer." (The "rubrics" are the direction or instructions presented in italics, which were traditionally printed in red.) Episcopalians are particular not only about the rubrics and ceremonies of common prayer, but also about the words and texts used. There is relatively little provision for individual, impromptu, public prayer.

Lutherans, on the other hand, although they are truly a liturgical church, have tended to be far more flexible and to allow for the insertion of much more in the way of personal and creative prayer, especially by the pastor. Lutherans have been united by their great common confession from Augsburg, 1530, often called after its Latin name, "Augustana." Whereas Episcopal clergy have been required to conform to the Book of Common Prayer, Lutherans have been required to subscribe to the Augsburg Confession. The liturgy does not have to carry as much of the burden of orthodoxy for Lutherans as it does for Episcopalians. So it is not surprising that Lutherans are sometimes irritated by what appears to be the excessive formality and rigidity of Episcopal worship. Episcopalians are, on the other hand, sometimes uncomfortable with the relative absence of regulation and the apparent impromptu, "off the cuff" nature of some Lutheran worship. This is a very broad generalization. There is much variety within each church and it is not unheard of to find a very formal, "high church" Lutheran congregation alongside a very "freed up," charismatic Episcopal parish.

Episcopalians are peculiar in that they use both a Prayer Book and a Hymnal. The Prayer Book contains no musical notation. Because much of the service may be sung, it is sometimes confusing to have to shift back and forth from one book to the other, often finding the same words in each, the Hymnal with musical notation and the Prayer Book without. The service music is usually very familiar to a congregation, so the visitor may notice that Episcopalians rarely pick up the Hymnal during a service. Typically, they follow the service in the Prayer Book, even though they may know it by heart, and use the Hymnal only to sing the hymns.

The stereotype is that Lutherans are more enthusiastic singers than Episcopalians. Anglicans have been strongly influenced by Puritanism, although they have stoutly resisted it. The Puritans were suspicious of hymns and sung services. To this day many Episcopalians consider the singing of the liturgy to be a "high church" practice and are surprised to find that the "very

Protestant" Lutherans routinely sing the services. In truth, one of the objections of the sixteenth century Reformers was to the medieval practice of "saying" a "low mass." Archbishop Cranmer's first Book of Common Prayer was intended for sung rather than said services, and it was "noted" for singing by John Merbecke. Luther's German Mass was intended to be sung in its entirety; even the canon (the prayer of consecration) was sung.

Going back far before the Reformation we find that Lutherans and Episcopalians have shared the great tradition of apostolic liturgies. We are heirs of the same ancient and medieval rites of Holy Baptism and Holy Eucharist. These rites were introduced into the British Isles at a very early period of Christian history. Later, the British Isles were the launching pad from which Celtic and Anglo-Saxon missionaries carried the faith to the Low Countries, Germany, and Scandinavia. Thus, the nations that were to become Lutheran learned Christian liturgy from British tutors.

On the other hand, the Reformation in England was born in the "German Club" that met at the White Horse Tavern in Cambridge to study "German" (i.e., Lutheran) theology. Before he became Archbishop of Canterbury, Thomas Cranmer, the great architect of the English Book of Common Prayer, studied in Germany and married the adopted daughter of Andreas Osiander, a leader of the Reformation in Germany. Cranmer was influenced by Luther's German Mass and by the liturgical thinking of the Lutheran Reformation.

Neither the Lutheran nor the Anglican heritage is that of a sect. It is important to remember that both came out of national church traditions. The Episcopal Church in the United States is the child of the Church of England. The Evangelical Lutheran Church in America is the offspring, or a least the grandchild, of national churches in Germany, Denmark, Sweden, Norway and other countries. Unlike a sect, a national church must be inclusive and provide for the religious needs of many. It must be comprehensive and accommodate various tastes, concerns, and points of view. So one finds in each of these denominations in America a wide variety of liturgical practices and an instinct to be accommodating. Keep in mind when visiting any particular Lutheran or Episcopal church that it may not be a typical church and that there are peculiarities or particularities about every time and place.

Lutherans and Episcopalians share common beliefs about the nature and efficacy of the sacraments, and both lay great stress on the chief sacraments: Holy Baptism and Holy Communion. However, Lutheran beliefs about these sacraments are held up and carried from generation to generation mainly by means of confession: that is doctrinal statements; principally the Augsburg Confession. Episcopal doctrine, on the other hand, is incorporated into liturgy: that is, the Common Prayer; by means of which it is preserved and passed on. Lutherans are uncomfortable with the fact that Episcopalians do not subscribe to or teach as necessary a formal, precise, and definitive doctrine of the Real Presence of Christ in the Holy Eucharist. Episcopalians, on the other hand, are sometimes offended by the relatively careless liturgical actions and words used by Lutherans in the celebration of Holy Communion. For example, how can one say that he believes in the real, objective presence of Christ in the elements of bread and wine and then carelessly pour the consecrated wine into hundreds of tiny glasses that will later be washed with detergent in a sink or dishwasher that empties into a public sewer? Perhaps Episcopalians need to learn to say and publish what they believe more clearly, as Lutherans have done, but it is highly doubtful that they ever will. Perhaps Lutherans need to learn to be more careful about how they act out their faith liturgically, but it is not likely that they will. Lutherans have grown accustomed to ample freedom and latitude in their modes of worship, and they are reluctant to impose rigid parameters on their clergy and people when it comes to liturgical practice. Episcopalians have grown accustomed to ample freedom and latitude in their theological perspectives and are reluctant to impose rigid parameters on their clergy and people when it comes to philosophical doctrinal statements. Neither of us is called to accept or reject the point of view of the other. Rather, we are called to mutual recognition. We are called to recognize God at work in one another. We are called to see Christ in one another. I am called to accept you as a Christian sister or brother, but I do not have to become like you in all ways. Our unity in Christ in the apostolic tradition we share transcends our differences.

Furthermore, we share a deep commitment to the visible worldwide Church as the Body of Christ, a living organism, a family into which one is born, an extension of the Incarnation and a bearer of God's grace. When confronted by congregationalists and others who see the Church as only a local assembly of believers, Lutherans and Episcopalians have always turned toward a more "high" and "catholic" doctrine of the Church. Certainly, both would agree and endorse the teaching of Richard Hooker who wrote:

> The Church is always a visible society of men; not an assembly, but a Society. For although the name of the Church be given unto Christian assemblies, although any multitude of Christian men congregated may be termed by the name of a Church, yet assemblies properly are rather things that belong to the Church. Men are assembled for performance of public actions; which actions being ended, the assembly dissolveth itself and is no longer in being, whereas the Church which was assembled doth no less continue afterwards than before.

> *Laws of Ecclesiastical Polity, Book III, Chapter 1*

Holy Baptism and Holy Communion are powerful signs of the societal nature of the Church and the means whereby we participate in that society. "In Holy Baptism God gives us new birth, adopts us as children, and makes us members of the body of Christ, the Church" (*The Use of the Means of Grace: A Statement on the Practice of Word and Sacrament*, paragraph S2.1, published by the ELCA, 1995). In the Episcopal baptismal rite the entire congregation proclaims, "We receive you into the household of God." The Episcopal Catechism lists among the benefits of Holy Communion "the strengthening of our union with Christ and one another." The Lutheran document cited, *The Use of the Means of Grace*, calls Holy Communion "a celebration of the Church, serving its unity" (S3.9).

A BIT OF AMERICAN HISTORY

Before we plunge into the texts, we need to take a quick look at the way the great evangelical catholic liturgical tradition was brought to America.

In English Colonial America the Prayer Book of the Church of England was in general use, principally the 1559 and 1662 recensions. This was true in the Colonies in which the use of the Prayer Book was permitted, but for a time its use was forbidden by the Puritans in Massachusetts and Connecticut. When Virginia's Assembly adopted the Declaration of Independence, one of the next orders of business was to disestablish the Church of England and to establish the Church of Virginia and revise the Prayer Book to take this change into account. Following the Revolution, the General Convention of the Episcopal Church, "far from intending to depart from the Church of England in any essential point of doctrine, discipline, or worship," (*Preface* to the Book of Common Prayer, 1789) prepared an American version of the Prayer Book. This version was the standard in the Episcopal Church in the United States for more than a century, suffering only minor revisions until 1892. In that year it was extensively revised to better serve the church under greatly changed circumstances. The next major revision, that of 1928, passed the General Convention only with the understanding that a liturgical commission would be established to complete the job of this revision, which was recognized to be inadequate. So, a Standing Liturgical Commission was formed. Its work was set aside, however, as the attention of the church was diverted by the Great Depression and the Second World War. It was not until 1950 that the Commission actually got about its assignment in a serious way. The Prayer Book was not revised and updated until 1979. The Book of Common Prayer and Administration of the Sacraments and Other Rites and Ceremonies of the Church According to the Use of the Episcopal Church (the full title of the Prayer Book), 1979, is the official standard liturgical book of the Episcopal Church in the United States today.

The transport of Lutheran liturgical traditions to America presents a vastly more complicated process. Here, to even begin to tell the story, we are faced with a plethora of ethnic and linguistic traditions: Swedish, German, Danish, Norwegian, Finnish, and more. None of these groups readily gave up their languages and religious customs in favor of Anglo-America. Each brought its own church order and "agenda," as the service books of these groups were most often called. The first English-language Lutheran liturgy in America was published in New York in 1795, but more than a century would pass before most Lutheran congregations had abandoned their native tongues for English in worship. A *Common Service in English* for use in various Lutheran judicatories and ethnic churches was finally published in 1888, and it was generally well received. This work was revised and expanded into the *Common Service Book* of 1917. The Lutheran Church-Missouri Synod published *The Lutheran Hymnal* in English in 1941. In 1958 the *Service Book and Hymnal* was published, and it became the accepted standard for most Lutheran bodies in America with the exception of the Missouri Synod. Finally, the publication of the *Lutheran Book of Worship* in 1978 and its acceptance by the major Lutheran groups, including both the Evangelical Lutheran Church in America (formerly the LCA and ALC) and the Lutheran Church-Missouri Synod, signaled a great day for corporate Christian worship among American Lutherans.

Like lightning across a dark sky, the tracers of the great evangelical catholic liturgy have brought light and energy to America. The first thing the first settlers at Jamestown did was to set up a crude table, spread a sail between two trees, and celebrate the Holy Communion, presided over by their chaplain, the Rev. Robert Hunt. By these rites Pocohontas was baptized and the conversion of her people began. The focus of the life of colonial New Sweden was on these baptismal and eucharistic liturgies. It was to Common Prayer that George Washington repaired that bitter winter at Valley Forge. In ante-bellum Virginia, Alabama, and elsewhere, these liturgies afforded many African-American slaves their only treatment to human dignity. It was to the communion liturgy that Robert E. Lee returned on that fateful Palm Sunday, 1865, at Appomattox. Upon receiving his orders to command the American Expeditionary Force, General Pershing's first act was to go to church where he and most of his staff received communion as a sort of viaticum for the journey which lay ahead. And when the Great War was over, the Senior Chaplain of the American Forces, Charles Henry Brent, and his European colleagues turned to the eucharistic liturgy for light and strength to found the movement which would become the World Council of Churches. Astronauts carried this liturgy into outer space and civil rights leaders used it as an instrument of corporate social protest when our government legally oppressed Black citizens in the South. These holy sacraments have been a witness to the presence of Christ in times of crisis through our country's history.

And so they stand today, ever changing to speak to changing times, and ever the same as the God they present is forever the same. Holy Baptism and Holy Communion are the direct and vital links that estranged and confused Americans have with their Creator. Through these instruments the God who is love embraces, energizes, and enlightens the spirits of his people.

THE
EUCHARISTIC
LITURGY

He interpreted to them the scriptures…
and made himself known to them in the breaking of bread.

Luke 24:27, 35

AN OUTLINE

	LBW Lutheran Book of Worship (Musical settings 1, 2, and 3, in order)	BCP Book of Common Prayer (Rite 1 and 2 listed in order)
Confession of Sin/ Penitential Rite	p. 56, p. 77, p. 98	p. 319, p. 351
Entrance Rite	p. 57, p. 78, p. 99	p. 323, p. 355

THE SPOKEN WORD
(Liturgy of the Word, Antecommunion, Pro-Anaphora, Mass of the Catechumens)

Lessons, Gospel, Sermon	p. 62, p. 82, p. 103	p. 325, p. 357
Creed	p. 64, p. 84, p. 105	p. 326, p. 358
Prayer and Peace	p. 65, p. 85, p. 106	p. 328, p. 359/383

THE SACRAMENTAL WORD
(Liturgy of the Table, Communion, Anaphora, Mass of the Faithful, Breaking of the Bread)

Offertory	p. 66, p. 86, p. 107	pp. 333/343, 361/376
Great Thanksgiving	p. 68, p. 88, p. 109	p. 333, p. 361
Our Father	p. 71, p. 91, p. 112	p. 336, p. 364
Breaking of the Bread	p. 71, p. 91, p. 114	p. 337, p. 364
Postcommunion Prayers	p. 72, p. 92, p. 115	p. 339, p. 365

Both traditions provide for the celebration of the Spoken Word without going on to the Sacramental Word. Neither allow for the celebration of the Sacramental Word without the Spoken Word.

The Liturgy of the Spoken Word derives from the old Jewish synagogue service. The Liturgy of the Sacramental Word is the sacred meal instituted by Jesus. It too has Jewish antecedent types.

(Note: In the selections from the LBW the people's parts will be in bold print.)	**A Penitential Order: Rite Two**

1)

BRIEF ORDER FOR CONFESSION AND FORGIVENESS	*For use at the beginning of the Liturgy, or as a separate service.*

A hymn, psalm, or anthem may be sung.

Stand

1. The minister leads the congregation in the invocation. The sign of the cross may be made by all in remembrance of their Baptism.

The people standing, the Celebrant says Blessed be God: Father, Son, and Holy Spirit.

People
And blessed be his kingdom, now

2)

In the name of the Father, and of the + Son, and of the Holy Spirit.

and for ever. Amen.

In place of the above, from Easter Day through the Day of Pentecost
Celebrant Alleluia. Christ is risen.
People **The Lord is risen indeed. Alleluia.**

Amen

Almighty God, to whom all hearts are open, all desires known, and from whom no secrets are hid: Cleanse the thoughts of our hearts by the inspiration of your Holy Spirit, that we may perfectly love you and worthily magnify your holy name, through Jesus Christ our Lord.

In Lent and on other penitential occasions
Celebrant Bless the Lord who forgives all our sins.
People **His mercy endures for ever.**

When used as a separate service, the Exhortation may be read, or a homily preached.

3)

Amen

The Decalogue may be said, the people kneeling.

4)

The Celebrant may read one of the following sentences

COMMENTARY

1) Both the Lutheran and Episcopal rites provide for an optional preparatory service of corporate confession of sin. This may stand on its own as a separate service, or it may be used at the very beginning of the communion liturgy.

2) According to Episcopal tradition only a bishop or priest may pronounce the absolution and forgiveness of sins, although a deacon or lay person may preside at this service when it is used as a separate service, modifying the absolution as directed by the rubrics. When the service immediately precedes the eucharist, the "celebrant," that is, the presiding priest or bishop, officiates. According to Lutheran tradition, only ordained clergy preside at this service. "Although it is true that any Christian may announce God's forgiveness to another, only the pastor may exercise the Office of the Keys in the gathered congregation" (*Manual on the Liturgy*, Augsburg, 1979, p. 188).

3) In the Lutheran rite Episcopalians will recognize the prayer that begins "Almighty God, to whom all hearts are open" as the familiar "Collect for Purity" with which virtually every Anglican communion rite has begun since 1549. The Latin prayer from which it is translated has been traced back to the eighth century court of Charlemagne and his famous Anglo-Saxon liturgist, Alcuin of York, who was probably its author.

4) The Episcopal Prayer Book Exhortation is referred to but not reproduced here. Interestingly, the Exhortation (page 316 in the Book of Common Prayer) derives from a German Lutheran source: the *Consultation of Herman*. Herman was an archbishop of Cologne who became a Lutheran. The *Consultation* is an invitation to self-examination and spiritual and ethical preparation

5)

If we say we have no sin, we deceive ourselves, and the truth is not in us. But if we confess our sins, God who is faithful and just will forgive our sins and cleanse us from all unrighteousness.

Kneel/Stand

2. Silence for reflection and self-examination

Jesus said, "The first commandment is this: Hear, O Israel: The Lord our God is the only Lord. Love the Lord your God with all your heart, with all your soul, with all your mind, and with all your strength. The second is this: Love your neighbor as yourself. There is no other commandment greater than these."
Mark 12:29-31

If we say that we have no sin, we deceive ourselves, and the truth is not in us. But if we confess our sins, God who is faithful and just, will forgive our sins and cleanse us from all unrighteousness.
John 1:8,9

The Deacon or Celebrant then says
Let us confess our sins against God and our neighbor.

6)   *Silence may be kept.*

Most merciful God,we confess that we are in bondage to sin and cannot free ourselves. We have sinned against you in thought, word, and deed, by what we have done and by what we have left undone. We have not loved our neighbors as ourselves. For the sake of your Son, Jesus Christ, have mercy on us. Forgive us, renew us, and lead us, so that we may delight in your will and walk in your ways, to the glory of your holy name. Amen.

Minister and People
Most merciful God, we confess that we have sinned against you in thought, word, and deed, by what we have done, and by what we have left undone. We have not loved you with our whole heart; we have not loved our neighbors as ourselves. We are truly sorry and we humbly repent. For the sake of your Son Jesus Christ, have mercy on us and forgive us; that we may delight in your will, and walk in your ways, to the glory of your Name. Amen.

for communion. Various English versions of this work have appeared in virtually all English and American Prayer Books since 1549.

5) Jesus' summary of the Law appears in all three synoptic Gospels: Matthew 22:37- 40, Luke 10: 27- 28, and Mark 12: 29- 31. The extensive use of the Decalogue (Ten Commandments) in the Church of England in the seventeenth century encouraged the rise of Sabbatarian sects, which attempted to follow the letter of the Mosaic Law. In Scottish and American Prayer Books the Episcopalians attempted to counter this trend with Jesus' famous Summary of the Law. It was well received and has been a part of every American Prayer Book since 1789.

6) The general, corporate prayers of repentance in each rite are remarkably similar, and each is followed by a very special prayer for the forgiveness of sins of those who are penitent. The Lutheran form of confession contains a reference to our "bondage to sin" which is reminiscent of some older Episcopal Prayer Book forms used at Morning and Evening Prayer in which it was said, for example, "There is no health in us." Such phrases reflect the classical Protestant doctrine of the depravity of mankind. General, public, confessions of sin were an innovation of the Reformation intended in the corporate spirit of the Lord's Prayer, "Forgive us our sins." This kind of acknowledgment of the social, communal, nature of sin was never intended to displace the confession of personal, individual sinfulness.

7)

3. The minister stand and addresses the congregation.

Almighty God, in his mercy, has given his Son to die for us and, for his sake, forgives us all our sins. As a called and ordained minister of the Church of Christ, and by his authority, I therefore declare to you the entire forgiveness of all your sins, in the name of the Father, and of the + Son, and of the Holy Spirit.

OR

In the mercy of almighty God, Jesus Christ was given to die for you and for his sake God forgives you all your sins. To those who believe in Jesus Christ he gives the power to become the children of God and bestows on them the Holy Spirit.

Amen

HOLY COMMUNION

1. The Brief Order for Confession and Forgiveness may be used before this service.

8)

2. The minister may announce the day and its significance before the Entrance Hymn, before the lessons, or at another appropriate time.

3. When there is no Communion, the service is concluded after the Creed as indicated.

The Bishop when present, or the Priest, stands and says

Almighty God have mercy on you, forgive you all your sins through our Lord Jesus Christ, strengthen you in all goodness, and by the power of the Holy Spirit keep you in eternal life. Amen.

A deacon or lay person using the preceding form substitutes "us" for "you" and "our" for "your."

When this Order is used at the beginning of the Liturgy, the service continues with the Gloria in excelsis, the Kyrie eleison, or the Trisagion.

When used separately, it concludes with suitable prayers and with the Grace or a blessing.

The Holy Eucharist: Rite Two

The Word of God

A hymn, psalm, or anthem may be sung.

7) Episcopalians call this prayer an "absolution," and it can be legitimately rendered only by a priest (presbyter) or bishop. Likewise, in the Lutheran tradition only a "minister" (i.e., an ordained pastor) pronounces this prayer, and in doing so the pastor is said to be exercising the "Office of the Keys" (see Matthew 16:19). In the Episcopal rite the absolution used in the eucharist is *precatory*: the priest prays that God will have mercy and forgive. In this prayer the second person "you" is plural. The Lutheran rite offers two prayers. The first may be interpreted as being *indicative*: the pastor is granting God's forgiveness by the authority given to called and ordained ministers. This type of absolution is found in the Book of Common Prayer in the rite for "The Reconciliation of a Penitent," pages 448 and 451, and in the proper liturgy for Ash Wednesday, page 269. The second prayer in the Lutheran Order is clearly *declaratory*: the minister is simply announcing that God forgives sin. Both churches use all three types of absolution or prayers of forgiveness in various services and under different circumstances: *precatory, indicative,* and *declaratory.*

8) Both communion liturgies may begin with a hymn or psalm, which is often sung in procession. Episcopalians are particularly fond of stirring ecclesiastical parades, "with the cross of Jesus going on before."

9)

Stand

4. The ENTRANCE HYMN or Psalm is sung.

5. The minister greets the congregation.

10)

The grace of our Lord Jesus Christ, the love of God, and the communion of the Holy Spirit be with you all.

And also with you.

6. The KYRIE may follow.

11)

In peace, let us pray to the Lord.
Lord, have mercy.

12)

For the peace from above, and for our salvation, let us pray to the Lord.
Lord, have mercy.

The people standing, the Celebrant says
Blessed be God: Father, Son, and Holy Spirit.
People
And blessed be his kingdom, now and for ever. Amen.

In place of the above, from Easter Day through the Day of Pentecost
Celebrant Alleluia. Christ is risen.
People **The Lord is risen indeed. Alleluia.**

In Lent and on other penitential occasions
Celebrant Bless the Lord who forgives all our sins.
People **His mercy endures for ever.**

The Celebrant may say
Almighty God, to you all hearts are open, all desires known, and from you no secrets are hid: Cleanse the thoughts of our hearts by the inspiration of your Holy Spirit, that we may perfectly love you, and worthily magnify your holy Name; through Christ our Lord.
Amen.

9) The opening greeting (salutation or acclamation) that is exchanged between the leader and the people is always the same in the Lutheran liturgy, but there are seasonal variations in the Episcopal rite. The greeting used in the Lutheran service is familiar to Episcopalians as the "Grace" at Morning and Evening Prayer. It appears in the New Testament in 2 Corinthians 13:13, and it is with this greeting that several of the ancient Christian liturgies began, for example, those of St. Clement and St. Basil. Likewise, the Episcopal acclamation has ancient and biblical precedents. It is reminiscent of the traditional Jewish and Christian greeting, "Blessed be God." In its present form it is lifted almost exactly from the *enarxis* (beginning) of the Greek Liturgy of St. John Chrysostom.

10) Notice that in Lutheran usage the term *minister* is used where Episcopalians use the term *celebrant*. Lutheran usage presumes that the *minister* will be an ordained pastor. The *Use of the Means of Grace* posits that "an ordained pastor presides in the service of Holy Communion and proclaims the Great Thanksgiving" (S3.9). In the Episcopal Church only bishops or priests may preside. Episcopalians use the term *celebrant* in its explicit dictionary, meaning "one who presides at a public religious rite." There is no intention of implying that the celebrant is the only person who *celebrates*, in the broader meaning of the word.

11) The prayer in the Episcopal liturgy that begins, "Almighty God, to you all hearts are open" is discussed earlier in comment 3.

12) From the early days of the church the Greek exclamatory prayer *Kyrie eleison* has been used by Christians in public worship. It is of pre-Christian origin and was an approximate Greek equivalent of the Jewish *hosanna*. It literally means "Lord, have mercy." Lutherans use an elaborate form of the *Kyrie*, which derives from the early medieval Greek liturgy of St. John Chrysostom (see comment 14).

For the peace of the whole world,
for the well-being of the Church of
God, and for the unity of all, let us
pray to the Lord.
Lord, have mercy.

For this holy house, and for all who
offer here their worship and praise,
let us pray to the Lord.
Lord, have mercy.

Help, save, comfort, and defend us,
gracious Lord.
Amen.

7. The HYMN OF PRAISE or another
appropriate hymn may be sung.

13)

Glory to God in the highest, and
peace to his people on earth.
Lord God, heavenly king, almighty
    God and Father:
We worship you, we give you thanks,
    we praise you for your glory.
Lord Jesus Christ, only Son of the
    Father,
Lord God, Lamb of God:
You take away the sin of the world;
    have mercy on us.
You are seated at the right hand of
    the Father; receive our prayer.
For you alone are the Holy One,
    you alone are the Lord,
    you alone are the Most High,
    Jesus Christ, with the Holy Spirit,
    in the glory of God the Father.
    Amen

When appointed, the following hymn
or some other song of praise is sung or
said, all standing

Glory to God in the highest,
    and peace to his people on
    earth.
Lord God, heavenly King,
    almighty God and Father,
        we worship you, we give you
        thanks, we praise you for
        your glory.
Lord Jesus Christ, only Son of the
    Father,
Lord God, Lamb of God,
    you take away the sin of the
    world:
        have mercy on us;
    you are seated at the right hand
    of the Father: receive our prayer.
For you alone are the Holy One,
you alone are the Lord,
you alone are the Most High,
    Jesus Christ, with the Holy
    Spirit, in the glory of God
    the Father. Amen.

13) The Lutheran "Hymn of Praise" is the same canticle that is called the *Gloria in excelsis* or "Glory to God in the highest." It is an elaboration on the angelic hymn at our Savior's birth (see Luke 2:14). It has served as an opening song of praise in the High Mass on Sundays and other major feast days since medieval times. Substitutions can and probably should be made from time to time, except during the Twelve Days of Christmas when it is particularly appropriate. The Book of Common Prayer proscribes its use during Lent and Advent (page 406). Among Lutherans, "This is the feast of victory for our God" (numbers 417 and 418 in the Episcopal *Hymnal*) is the most popular substitute. It is a paraphrase of Revelation 5:12-13. Episcopalians often use the *Te Deum laudamas*, "You are God" (Book of Common Prayer, page 95), or, during the Easter season the *Pascha nostrum*, "Christ Our Passover" (Book of Common Prayer, page 83). The *Quaerite Dominum*, "The Second Song of Isaiah," and *Kyrie Pantokrator*, "A Song of Penitence" (Book of Common Prayer, pages 86 and 90, respectively), are particularly appropriate for Lent.

OR
This is the feast of victory for our
    God.
        Alleluia, alleluia, alleluia.
Worthy is Christ, the Lamb who
    was slain, whose blood set us
    free to be people of God.

On other occasions the following is used

14)

Lord, have mercy   or   Kyrie eleison

Christ, have mercy   or   Christe eleison

Lord, have mercy   or   Kyrie eleison

or this

15)

Holy God,
Holy and Mighty,
Holy Immortal One,
Have mercy upon us.

16)

8. The PRAYER OF THE DAY is said;
the salutation may precede it.

The Collect of the Day

The Celebrant says to the people

The Lord be with you.

The Lord be with you.

And also with you.

People **And also with you.**

Let us pray.

Celebrant Let us pray.
The Celebrant says the Collect.

Amen

People **Amen.**

14) Comment 12 mentions the Lutheran use of the *Kyrie*. Episcopalians use it in lieu of the *Gloria in excelsis* on weekdays and in penitential seasons. Actually, this Episcopal practice probably reflects a somewhat distorted understanding of the nature of the ancient exclamation, *Kyrie eleison*, which may be the result of Cranmer's sixteenth century translation of the phrase as "Lord, have mercy upon us." That translation tended to be read as having a somber, heavy, penitential tone which actually is not present in Greek usage and is largely avoided in the Lutheran liturgy. The printed text in the Book of Common Prayer is that of the threefold *Kyrie*, but a ninefold version is often sung. Inasmuch as the Greek exclamation does not lend itself to a succinct translation, the use of the original Greek is permitted.

15) One of the most ancient and powerful hymn/prayers of the church is the majestic *Trisagion*, "Holy God, Holy and Mighty." Like the *Kyrie*, it may be said or sung antiphonally, threefold, or simply as printed. The *Trisagion* is of Greek origin and was an important part of the old Celtic and Gallican rites in Western Europe and the British Isles. The medieval Latin rites always used it on Good Friday. Reformation rites, both Lutheran and Anglican, used it at funerals. The Episcopal Prayer Book has restored this prayer to its ancient place in the eucharistic liturgy, using it as a hymn in the entrance rite. Lutherans use it in their formal suffrages: Responsive Prayers 1 and 2 in the *Lutheran Book of Worship*, pages 161 and 164 respectively.

16) What Lutherans call the "Prayer of the Day," Episcopalians call the "Collect of the Day." (In the English noun *collect*, the emphasis is on the first syllable. It refers to a prayer that is used to call an assembly together.) Because the two churches share essentially the same calendar, these prayers are often identical. Both churches have always used the traditional greeting and invitation to prayer: *Dominus vobiscum/Et cum spiritu tuo/Oremus*

17)

Sit	**The Lessons**

9. The FIRST LESSON is announced and read.

The First Lesson is from the ___ chapter of ___.

The people sit. One or two Lessons, as appointed, are read, the Reader first saying

A Reading (Lesson) from ___.

10. After the lesson the reader may say: "Here ends the reading."

A citation giving chapter and verse may be added.

11. The appointed PSALM is sung or said.

After each Reading, the Reader may say

The Word of the Lord.

12. The SECOND LESSON is announced and read.

People **Thanks be to God.**

The Second Lesson is from the ___ chapter of ___.

Or the Reader may say

Here ends the Reading (Epistle)

13. After the lesson the reader may say: "Here ends the reading."

Silence may follow.

14. The appointed VERSE is sung by the choir, or the congregation may sing the appropriate Verse below:

A Psalm, hymn, or anthem may follow each Reading.

Stand

**Alleluia. Lord, to whom shall we go?
You have the words of eternal life.
Alleluia. Alleluia.**

LENT

**Return to the Lord, your God,
    for he is gracious and merciful,
    slow to anger,
    and abounding in steadfast love.**

in the Latin mass. In English: "The Lord be with you." "And also with you." (literally, "And with your spirit.") "Let us pray."

17) The custom and pattern of Bible reading at this point in the service are not only shared by Lutherans and Episcopalians, but are typical of Roman Catholic and Eastern Orthodox churches the world over, deriving from the very earliest Christian liturgies. The basic pattern of lessons and psalms is borrowed from the liturgical practices of the Jewish synagogues in Jesus' day and earlier. First there is a lesson from the Old Testament, and a psalm is sung or read. Then there is a lesson from the New Testament, usually from an epistle. In both churches today it is most common for the congregation to sit for these lessons. Lutherans and Episcopalians share a nearly identical Sunday lectionary, so the lessons read in the churches are usually the same. We also share an identical version of the Psalter. The reading and singing of psalms has always been a significant part of orthodox Christian piety, although Christians must interpret them metaphorically in order to use them devotionally. References to the king become references to Jesus, Christ the King; Jerusalem comes to signify the church, the city of God; and so forth. The translation of the Psalms now used in both churches is a contemporary revision of the Coverdale Psalter which was published in the Great Bible in England in 1539. It was revised for the 1979 Book of Common Prayer but actually adopted first by Lutherans in the 1978 *Lutheran Book of Worship*. It is set out in lines of poetry that correspond to Hebrew versification, which is not based on meter or rhyme but on parallelism of clauses, a symmetry of form and sense rather than of sound or rhythm. This fresh translation has generally been judged as elegant, pleasing, and accurate: a gem of biblical/liturgical scholarship. The psalms are said or sung in a variety of ways in both churches: in unison, antiphonally, responsively, and so on. Explicit directions for the public reading of psalms is found on page 582 of the Book of Common Prayer.

18)

15. *The GOSPEL is announced.*	*Then, all standing, the Deacon or a Priest reads the Gospel, first saying*
The Holy Gospel according to St.___, the ___ chapter.	The Holy Gospel of our Lord Jesus Christ according to ___.
Glory to you, O Lord.	*People* **Glory to you, Lord Christ.**
16. *After the reading the minister may say:* "*The Gospel of the Lord.*"	*After the Gospel, the Reader says*
Praise to you, O Christ.	The Gospel of the Lord.
	People **Praise to you, Lord Christ**

17. *The Hymn of the Day may be sung before the sermon.*

Sit.

18. *The SERMON. Silence for reflection may follow.*

The Sermon

19)

19. *The HYMN OF THE DAY is sung.*

20. *The CREED may be said. The Nicene Creed is said on all festivals and on Sundays in the seasons of Advent, Christmas, Lent, and Easter. The Apostles' Creed is said at other times. The Creed is omitted here if the service of Holy Baptism or another rite with a creed is used.*

On Sunday and other Major Feasts there follows, all standing

18) In both traditions the reading of the Gospel is the climax of the Scripture lessons, and it is one of the principal ways that Jesus Christ makes himself known in the liturgy. The Gospel is normally read by someone in holy orders, traditionally a deacon in those churches that have deacons. Often it is framed with special music, and the people always stand. It may be read from the pulpit where the sermon is about to be preached, or it may be ceremonially carried into "the midst of the congregation" and read from there. The Sermon, which follows, is mandatory in both rites, and it is presumed that it will be based on the Scriptures that have just been read.

19) Lutherans have an ingenious plan that gives each Sunday and major festival appointed hymns or a "Hymn of the Day." See page 929 of the *Lutheran Book of Worship*. This hymn deals with the themes of the prescribed Scripture lessons and should be related to the sermon. It can either precede or follow the sermon.

20)

NICENE CREED

The Nicene Creed

We believe in one God, the Father, the Almighty, maker of heaven and earth, of all that is, seen and unseen.

We believe in one Lord, Jesus Christ, the only Son of God, eternally begotten of the Father, God from God, Light from Light, true God from true God, begotten, not made, of one Being with the Father. Through him all things were made. For us and for our salvation he came down from heaven: by the power of the Holy Spirit he became incarnate from the Virgin Mary, and was made man. For our sake he was crucified under Pontius Pilate; he suffered death and was buried. On the third day he rose again in accordance with the Scriptures; he ascended into heaven and is seated at the right hand of the Father. He will come again in glory to judge the living and the dead, and his kingdom will have no end.

We believe in the Holy Spirit, the Lord, the giver of life, who proceeds from the Father and the Son. With the Father and the Son he is worshipped and glorified. He has spoken through the Prophets. We believe in one holy catholic and apostolic Church. We acknowledge one baptism for the forgiveness of sins.We look for the resurrection of the dead, and the life of the world to come. Amen

We believe in one God, the Father, the Almighty, maker of heaven and earth, of all that is, seen and unseen.

We believe in one Lord, Jesus Christ, the only Son of God, eternally begotten of the Father, God from God, Light from Light, true God from true God, begotten, not made of one Being with the Father. Through him all things were made. For us and for our salvation he came down from heaven: by the power of the Holy Spirit he became incarnate from the Virgin Mary, and was made man. For our sake he was crucified under Pontius Pilate; he suffered death and was buried. On the third day he rose again in accordance with the Scriptures; he ascended into heaven and is seated at the right hand of the Father. He will come again in glory to judge the living and the dead, and his kingdom will have no end.

We believe in the Holy Spirit, the Lord, the giver of life, who proceeds from the Father and the Son. With the Father and the Son he is worshipped and glorified. He has spoken through the Prophets. We believe in one holy catholic and apostolic Church. We acknowledge one baptism for the forgiveness of sins. We look for the resurrection of the dead, and the life of the world to come. Amen.

20) The Nicene Creed is customarily used by both Lutherans and Episcopalians on Sundays and major festivals. This is the Creed of the Councils of Nicaea and Constantinople. It is sometimes called the "Universal Creed," inasmuch as it was received as authoritative by virtually the whole church throughout the world after A.D. 381. It was probably first used in the eucharistic liturgy after the Gospel (and sermon) in Antioch in the fifth century. This use of the Nicene Creed spread through the Eastern churches and was introduced into the West in the sixth century. It is one of the fundamental ecumenical documents on which Lutheran/Episcopal intercommunion is based. Both rites have provision for the alternative use of the Apostles' Creed in the eucharistic liturgy at some times. (The Apostles' Creed is the ancient baptismal creed of Rome. We will take a closer look at it when we consider Holy Baptism.) Furthermore, the Athanasian Creed is accepted by both churches; it is printed in both the *Lutheran Book of Worship* (page 54) and in the Book of Common Prayer (page 864). It is a tradition in both churches to read this exquisite theological document in the liturgy on Trinity Sunday. But that is the only time it is used liturgically.

21. When there is no Communion, the service continues on page __.

21)

22. THE PRAYERS are said.

Let us pray for the whole people of God in Christ Jesus, and for all people according to their needs.

Prayers are included for the whole Church, the nations, those in need, the parish, special concerns.

The congregation may be invited to offer petitions and thanksgivings.

Prayer of confession may be included if the Brief Order for Confession and Forgiveness has not been used earlier.

22)

The minister gives thanks for the faithful departed, especially for those who recently have died.

After each portion of the prayers:

Lord, in your mercy, OR Let us pray
 to the Lord.
Hear our prayer   Lord, have mercy

The prayers conclude:

Into your hands, O Lord, we commend all for whom we pray, trusting in your mercy; through your Son, Jesus Christ our Lord.

Amen

The Prayers of the People

*Prayer is offered with intercession for
The Universal Church, its members,
 and its mission
The Nation and all in authority
The welfare of the world
The concerns of the local community
Those who suffer and those in any trouble
The departed (with commemoration of
 a saint when appropriate)*

See forms beginning on page__.

*If there is no celebration of the Communion
or if a priest is not available, the service
is concluded as directed on page__.*

Confession of Sin

A Confession of Sin is said here if it has not been said earlier. On occasion, the Confession may be omitted.

The Deacon or Celebrant says
Let us confess our sins against God and our neighbor.

Silence may be kept.

Minister and People
**Most merciful God,
we confess that we have sinned
against you in thought, word, and
deed, by what we have done,
and by what we have left undone.
   We have not loved our neighbor
      as ourselves. We are truly sorry
         and we humbly repent. For the
   sake of your Son Jesus Christ, have
      mercy on us and forgive us; that**

21) What Episcopalians call "The Prayers of the People" (or "The Prayer for the Whole State of Christ's Church") Lutherans call the "Prayer of the Church" or simply "The Prayers." Both liturgies make provision for more or less free intercessions at this point. However, in practice Episcopalians almost always use one of the set forms (I through VI, pages 383-393 of the Book of Common Prayer). Lutherans may use the "Prayer of the Church," which appears on page 52f of the *Lutheran Book of Worship*. There is a strong tradition of "the pastoral prayer" in the Sunday service among Protestants, including Lutherans. This is a long prayer, composed and delivered by the pastor, which summarizes the particular desires and petitions of the congregation. Lutherans have retained this, in essence, while providing for congregational participation in each portion of the pastor's prayer. The pastor ends each portion or segment with a cue ("Lord, in your mercy" or "Let us pray to the Lord"), to which the people have a response ("Hear our prayer" or "Lord, have mercy"). Both traditions are quite clear about the areas of concern for which prayers are to be offered.

22) Lutherans may insert a Confession of Sin in the Prayers if the Order for Confession and Forgiveness has not been used earlier. Episcopalians most frequently use the Confession of Sin and Absolution, which appears here in lieu of the Penitential Order before the eucharistic liturgy.

we may delight in your will, and
walk in your ways, to the glory of
your Name. **Amen.**

*The Bishop when present, or the Priest,
stands and says*
Almighty God have mercy on you,
forgive you all your sins through our
Lord Jesus Christ, strengthen you in
all goodness, and by the power of
the Holy Spirit keep you in eternal
life. **Amen.**

23)

*23. The PEACE is shared at this time
or after the Lord's Prayer, prior to the
distribution.*

The Peace
*(If preferred, the exchange of the Peace
may take place at the time of the
administration of the Sacrament.)*

*All stand. The Celebrant says to the
people*

The peace of the Lord be with you
always.

The peace of the Lord be always
with you.

And also with you.

People   **And also with you.**

*The ministers and congregation may
greet one another in the name of the
Lord.*

*Then the Ministers and People may
greet one another in the name of the
Lord.*

Peace be with you.
Peace be with you.

23) Biblical scholars find no less than a dozen references to the exchange of "The Peace" (sometimes "kiss of peace") in the New Testament. It was a part of the eucharistic ritual of the early church; a reenactment of the scene described in Luke 24:36-43 and a way of celebrating the sacramental presence of the risen Lord. The custom remained in Christian liturgies of the East and West until late medieval times; after which it was observed only by the officiating clergy if observed at all. It has been recovered for the people in this century, although sometimes in a debased form, as no more than a time to visit and chat with those around you. Both Lutheran and Episcopal rites provide an alternative place for The Peace in the liturgy: just prior to the distribution of communion. However, it is most often exchanged as a particularly fitting conclusion to the Liturgy of the Word and the Prayers. In early Christian liturgies this was the time for visitors, the catechumens, and those who were excommunicated, to leave. The rest of the service, sometimes called the "Mass of the Faithful," was open only to those who were baptized and in good standing. This is a natural and appropriate break in the flow of the liturgy, and announcements are often made here.

24)

24. The OFFERING is received as the Lord's table is prepared.

25. The appointed OFFERTORY may be sung by the choir as the gifts are presented, or the congregation may sing one of the following offertories, or an appropriate hymn or psalm may be sung.
25)

Let the vineyards be fruitful, Lord,
  and fill to the brim our cup of
  blessing,
Gather a harvest from the seeds
  that were sown, that we may be
  fed with the bread of life.
Gather the hopes and the dreams
  of all; unite them with the
  prayers we offer now.
Grace our table with your presence,
  and give us a foretaste of the
  feast to come.

What shall I render to the Lord for
  all his benefits to me?
I will offer the sacrifice of thanks
  giving and will call on the name
  of the Lord.
I will take the cup of salvation and
  will call on the name of the Lord.
I will pay my vow to the Lord now
  in the presence of his people,
in the courts of the Lord's house,
  in the midst of you, O Jerusalem.

The Holy Communion

The Celebrant may begin the Offertory with one of the sentences on page __, or with some other sentence of Scripture.

(Offertory Sentences

Offer to God a sacrifice of thanksgiving, and make good your vows to the Most High. *Psalm 50:14*

Ascribe to the Lord the honor due his Name; bring offerings and come into his courts. *Psalm 96:8*

Walk in love, as Christ loved us and gave himself for us, an offering and a sacrifice to God. *Ephesians 5:2*

I appeal to you, brethren, by the mercies of God, to present yourselves as a living sacrifice, holy and acceptable to God, which is your spiritual worship. *Romans 12:1*

If you are offering your gift at the altar, and there remember that your brother has something against you, leave your gift there before the altar and go; first be reconciled to your brother, and then come and offer your gift. *Matthew 5:23,24*

Through Christ let us continually offer to God the sacrifice of praise, that is, the fruit of lips that acknowledge his Name. But do not neglect to do good and to share what you have, for such sacrifices are pleasing to God. *Hebrews 13:15,16*

Lord our God, you are worthy to receive glory and honor and power; because you have created all things, and by your will they were created and have their being. *Revelation 4:11*

24) Dom Gregory Dix, an Anglican Benedictine, was one of the great liturgical scholars of this century. In his classic work, *The Shape of the Liturgy*, he had the following strong words to say about the eucharistic liturgy of the early church:

> With absolute unanimity the liturgical tradition reproduces these actions
>
> 1. The offertory; bread and wine are taken and placed on the table together.
>
> 2. The prayer; the president gives thanks to God over bread and wine together.
>
> 3. The fraction; the bread is broken.
>
> 4. The communion; the bread and wine are distributed together.
>
> In that form and in that order these four actions constituted the absolutely invariable nucleus of every eucharistic rite known to us throughout antiquity from the Euphrates to Gaul.

Lutheran and Episcopal communion rites adhere to this ancient, apostolic pattern.

25) In the eucharistic liturgy of both the Episcopal and Lutheran traditions the offertory is much more than the taking of a "collection" of money. The elements of bread and wine are taken to the holy table, and the people are called upon to offer themselves to the service of God. In the *Lutheran Book of Worship*, Lutherans have more explicit and elaborate liturgical resources for the offertory than do Episcopalians. "Let the vineyards be fruitful" and "What shall I render to the Lord" are noted for singing and printed in the service book itself in this place.

26. After the gifts have been presented, one of these prayers is said.
Let us pray.

Merciful Father, **we offer with joy and thanksgiving what you have first given us our selves, our time, and our possessions, signs of your gracious love. Receive them for the sake of him who offered himself for us, Jesus Christ our Lord. Amen**

Blessed are you, **O Lord our God, maker of all things. Through your goodness you have blessed us with these gifts. With them we offer ourselves to your service and dedicate our lives to the care and redemption of all that you have made, for the sake of him who gave himself for us, Jesus Christ our Lord. Amen**

27. The ministers make ready the bread and wine.

26)

28. The GREAT THANKSGIVING is begun by the minister standing at the altar.

The Lord be with you.

And also with you.

Lift up your hearts.

We lift them to the Lord.

Let us give thanks to the Lord our God.

It is right to give him thanks and praise.

Yours, O Lord, is the greatness, the power the glory, the victory, and the majesty. For everything in heaven and on earth is yours. Yours, O Lord, is the kingdom, and you are exalted as head over all.
I Chronicles 29:11)

During the Offertory, a hymn, psalm, or anthem may be sung.

Representatives of the congregation bring the people's offerings of bread and wine, and money or other gifts, to the deacon or celebrant. The people stand while the offerings are presented and placed on the Altar.

The Great Thanksgiving

The people remain standing. The Celebrant, whether bishop or priest, faces them and sings or says

The Lord be with you.
People   **And also with you.**
Celebrant Lift up your hearts.
People   **We lift them to the Lord.**
Celebrant Let us give thanks to the
              Lord our God.
People   **It is right to give him
              thanks and praise.**

26) The prayers and actions that come now in the service have long been called the *canon* of the mass. *Canon* is a Greek word that means "rule" or "standard," among other things. In Western Christendom this prayer has long been regarded as *sine qua non* of the communion liturgy. From the early days of the church the Invitation to the Thanksgiving (Latin, *Sursum corda*), a Preface, and the Thrice Holy Hymn (Latin, *Sanctus*) have constituted a climactic act of praise in the Christian eucharistic liturgy. The sentence, "Let us give thanks to the Lord our God," (Greek, *Eucharistesomen toi Kirioi*) is an invitation to the people of God to offer the eucharist (the Thanksgiving/Holy Communion). This is the ancient and universal way that the invitation to participate in the sacred meal is phrased. The ancient response of the people, "It is right to do so" (Greek, *Axion kai dikaion*), is a formal way of giving consent. Neither Lutherans nor Episcopalians allow a pastor/priest to celebrate the eucharist alone, without the consent and participation of a congregation. To do so would reduce the sacred meal of the gathered community to the level of a mere private devotion. Both rites have proper "Prefaces," introductory declamations that precede the climactic "Holy, Holy, Holy" and are appropriate to the day or season. A proper Preface usually makes reference to Isaiah's vision of the angelic heavenly host and invites the people to join in singing the *Sanctus*. Martin Luther liked to point out the scriptural origin of this great hymn (Isaiah 6:3), and he prepared music and a text for his German Mass that began, "Isaiah the Prophet in a vision of old" (*Jesaja dem Prophetem*). This appears today as number 528 in the *Lutheran Book of Worship*.

29. The preface appropriate to the day or season is sung or said.

It is indeed right and salutary . . . we praise you name and join their unending hymn:

Then, facing the Holy Table, the Celebrant proceeds

It is right, and a good and joyful thing, always and everywhere to give thanks to you, Father Almighty, Creator of heaven and earth.

Here a Proper Preface is sung or said on all Sundays, and on other occasions as appointed.

Therefore we praise you, joining our voices with Angels and Archangels and with all the company of heaven, who forever sing this hymn to proclaim the glory of your Name:

Celebrant and People

**Holy, holy, holy Lord, God of power and might:
Heaven and earth are full of your glory.
Hosanna in the highest.
Blessed is he who comes in the name of the Lord.
Hosanna in the highest.**

**Holy, holy, holy Lord, God of power and might, heaven and earth are full of your glory.
Hosanna in the highest.
Blessed is he who comes in the name of the Lord.
Hosanna in the highest.**

The people stand or kneel.

30. The minister continues

Then the Celebrant continues

27)

31. The minister may say:

Holy God, mighty Lord, gracious Father: Endless is your mercy and eternal your reign.

You have filled all creation with light and life; heaven and earth are full of your glory.

Holy and gracious Father: In your infinite love you made us for yourself; and, when we had fallen into sin and become subject to evil and death, you, in your mercy, sent Jesus Christ, your only and eternal Son, to share our human nature, to live and die as one of us, to reconcile us to you, the God and Father of all.

27) In English this part of the Canon is customarily called the "Prayer of Consecration" or the "Eucharistic Prayer." The *Lutheran Book of Worship* (pew edition) provides three forms. The *Book of Common Prayer* provides four. Here we reproduce only one of the options in each rite.

28) The canon customarily includes an *anamnesis*. An *anamnesis* is literally "a remembering," but the term in ecclesiastical (New Testament/*koine*) Greek is much stronger. It means to take something from the past and make it present in the here and now. We turn to the bread and wine and recall Jesus' Last Supper with his disciples, in which he instituted the eucharistic meal and commanded its observance: "Do this in remembrance of me." We also recall his mighty saving acts on the cross and his victory over death. He makes himself present in the breaking of the bread, and we receive him as our spiritual and physical nourishment. The early church sometimes recalled the "Feeding of the Five Thousand" or the experience of the disciples on the road to Emmaus in addition to or in lieu of the recollection of the "Last Supper." In the liturgy of the medieval Latin church the words of Jesus that were repeated by the priest over the communion bread were *"Hoc est enim corpus meum"* (This is my body) and *"Hic est enim calix sanguinis"* (This is my blood). To some of the faithful these precise words appeared to

Through Abraham you promised to
bless all nations. You rescued
Israel, your chosen people.

Through the prophets you renewed
your promise; and, at this end of
all the ages, you sent your Son,
who in words and deeds proclaimed your kingdom and was
obedient to your will, even to giving his life.

28)

In the night in which he was
betrayed, our Lord Jesus took
bread, and gave thanks, broke it,
and gave it to his disciples saying:
Take and eat; this is my body,
given for you.

Do this for the remembrance of me.

Again, after supper, he took the cup,
gave thanks, and gave it for all to
drink, saying: This cup is the new
covenant in my blood, shed for
you and for all people for the forgiveness of sin.

Do this for the remembrance of me.

For as often as we eat of this bread
and drink from this cup, we proclaim the Lord's death until he
comes.

Christ has died.

Christ is risen.

Christ will come again.

He stretched out his arms upon the
cross, and offered himself in obedience to your will, a perfect sacrifice
for the whole world.

*At the following words concerning the
bread, the Celebrant is to hold it, or lay
a hand upon it; and at the words concerning the cup, to hold or place a
hand upon the cup and any other vessel
containing wine to be consecrated.*

On the night he was handed over to
suffering and death, our Lord Jesus
Christ took bread; and when he had
given thanks to you, he broke it,
and gave it to his disciples, and said,
"Take, eat: This is my Body, which is
given for you. Do this for the
remembrance of me."

After supper he took the cup of
wine; and when he had given
thanks, he gave it to them, and said,
"Drink this, all of you: This is my
Blood of the new Covenant, which
is shed for you and for many for the
forgiveness of sins.
Whenever you drink it, do this for
the remembrance of me."

Therefore we proclaim the mystery
of faith:

Celebrant and People

Christ has died.

Christ is risen.

Christ will come again.

have a sort of magical power, and an overwhelming emphasis was placed on their utterance. Protestant liturgists of the sixteenth century, and Roman Catholic liturgists of the twentieth, have sought to discourage this. The early church and the Eastern churches have always seen the Consecration in the broader context of the entire service. Christ makes himself present and known in the gathered community when the Word is spoken and the Bread is broken. Liturgical reformers have recovered a strong "Institution Narrative" in which the story of our creation and redemption is recalled. As it now stands, we have fairly elaborate Institution Narratives and Prayers of Consecration which place the consecration of the bread and wine firmly in context. They conclude with the Memorial Acclamations: "Christ has died. Christ is risen. Christ will come again." Such acclamations were common among some of the ancient Eastern liturgies but they are a twentieth century addition to Western ones. They provide an enrichment which has been well received.

Therefore, gracious Father, with this bread and cup we remember the life our Lord offered for us.	*The Celebrant continues*
	We celebrate the memorial of our redemption, O Father, in this sacrifice of praise and thanksgiving. Recalling his death, resurrection, and ascension, we offer you these gifts.
And, believing the witness of his resurrection, we await his coming in power to share with us the great and promised feast.	

Amen. Come, Lord Jesus. 29)

Send now, we pray, your Holy Spirit, the spirit of our Lord and of his resurrection, that we who receive the Lord's body and blood may live to the praise of your glory and receive our inheritance with all your saints in light.

Sanctify them by your Holy Spirit to be for your people the Body and Blood of your Son, the holy food and drink of new and unending life in him. Sanctify us also that we may faithfully receive this holy Sacrament, and serve you in unity, constancy, and peace; and at the last day bring us with all your saints into the joy of your eternal kingdom. All this we ask through your Son Jesus Christ. By him, and with him, and in him, in the unity of the Holy Spirit all honor and glory is yours, Almighty Father, now and for ever.

Amen. Come, Holy Spirit.

Join our prayers with those of your servants of every time and every place, and unite them with the ceaseless petitions of our great high priest until he comes as victorious Lord of all.

AMEN.

Through him, with him, in him, in the unity of the Holy Spirit, all honor and glory is yours, almighty Father, now and forever. Amen

As our Savior Christ has taught us, we now pray,

Our Father in heaven, 30)
    hallowed be your name,
    your kingdom come,
    your will be done,
        on earth as in heaven.
Give us today our daily bread.
Forgive us our sins
    as we forgive those
    who sin against us.
	Our Father in heaven,
	    hallowed be your name,
	    your kingdom come,
	    your will be done,
	        on earth as in heaven.
	Give us today our daily bread.
	Forgive us our sins
	    as we forgive those
	    who sin against us.

29) The canon also customarily includes an *epiclesis* (invocation of the Holy Spirit). Here we invoke the Spirit of God to descend upon the elements of bread and wine and upon us who will receive them. The Lutheran liturgy incorporates into the *epiclesis* the ancient Christian *maranatha* "Come, Lord Jesus" (Revelation 22:20).

30) The canon traditionally ends with the Lord's Prayer. Both Lutheran and Episcopal liturgies provide for the use of the contemporary English translation of this prayer, the text approved by the International Consultation on English Texts (ICET), a consortium of English-speaking Roman Catholic, Lutheran, and Anglican scholars. (The *Episcopal Prayer Book* also allows for the use of the translation that appeared in the 1789 American *Book of Common Prayer* and in subsequent American versions which is sometimes called the "familiar" or "traditional" translation. It begins, "Our Father, who art in heaven." Contrary to popular notion that is neither the form of the Lord's Prayer that appears in the King James Version of the Bible nor the one used in older Prayer Books.)

LBW	BCP

Save us from the time of trial
  and deliver us from evil.
For the kingdom, the power,
  and the glory are yours,
  now and for ever. Amen.
	Save us from the time of trial
	  and deliver us from evil.
	For the kingdom, the power,
	  and the glory are yours,
	  now and for ever. Amen.

31)

Sit	**The Breaking of the Bread**
34. *The COMMUNION follows. The bread may be broken for distribution.*	*The Celebrant breaks the consecrated Bread.*
35. *The presiding minister and the assisting ministers receive the bread and wine and then give them to those who come to receive. As the ministers give the bread and wine, they say these words to each communicant:*	*A period of silence is kept.* *Then may be sung or said* [Alleluia.] Christ our Passover is sacrificed for us; **Therefore let us keep the feast. [Alleluia.]**
The body of Christ, given for you.	*In Lent, Alleluia is omitted, and may be omitted at other time except during Easter Season.*
The blood of Christ, shed for you.	
36. *The communicant may say: "Amen."*	*In place of, or in addition to, the preceding, some other suitable anthem may be used.*
37. *Hymns and other music may be used during the ministration of Communion. One of the hymns may be the following.*	*The following anthem may be used at the Breaking of the Bread:*

Lamb of God, you take away the sin of the world;
    have mercy on us.
Lamb of God, you take away the sin of the world;
    have mercy on us.
Lamb of God, you take away the sin of the world;
    grant us peace.
	Lamb of God, you take away the sin of the world;
	    have mercy on us.
	Lamb of God, you take away the sin of the world;
	    have mercy on us.
	Lamb of God, you take away the sin of the world;
	    grant us peace.

31) The eucharistic meal is referred to in Holy Scripture as "the breaking of the bread" (Acts 2:42, 20:7; 1 Corinthians 10:16 - 17; etc.). In the ancient and medieval Western church it was customary to make a significant display of the act of breaking the consecrated bread, called the "Fraction." Although the bread is usually broken in a moment of reverent silence, at least three anthems have been associated with this liturgical action in past centuries: *Pascha nostrum* (Christ Our Passover), *Sancta sanctis* (Holy things for holy ones), and *Agnus Dei* (Lamb of God). The first two are incorporated into the Episcopal rite as "Christ our Passover is sacrificed for us" and "The Gifts of God for the People of God," and the third is often used as a post Fraction hymn in both rites. In medieval and Renaissance times in the Western church elaborate acts of adoration of the elements at this point often replaced the administration of communion to the people. This led the English Reformers to write in the Thirty-Nine Articles of Religion: "The Sacraments were not ordained of Christ to be gazed upon, or to carried about, but that we should duly use them." And again, "The Sacrament of the Lord's Supper was not by Christ's ordinance reserved, carried about, lifted up, or worshipped." Rather, Christ's command was to "take, eat" and "drink." The Reformers were not denying the Real Presence of Christ in the sacrament, or the practice of taking communion to the sick who could not attend the eucharist. On the contrary, they were advocating that the faithful be allowed to obey Christ's command to receive him sacramentally. This was classical Protestantism, as well as orthodox Catholicism. However, it led to the elimination of the Elevation and the diminution of the Fraction among Protestants. But it also led to the regular administration of communion to the faithful in "both kinds," that is the restoration of the cup to the laity.

Stand	*Facing the people, the Celebrant says the following Invitation*
38. After all have returned to their places, the minister may say these or similar words.	The Gifts of God for the People of God.
The body and blood of our Lord Jesus Christ strengthen you and keep you in his grace. **Amen**	*And may add* Take them in remembrance that Christ died for you, and feed on him in your hearts by faith with thanksgiving.
	The ministers receive the Sacrament in both kind, and then immediately deliver it to the people.

32)

39. The POST-COMMUNION canticle or an appropriate hymn is sung as the table is cleared.	*The Bread and Cup are given to the communicants with these words*
Thank the Lord and sing his praise; tell everyone what he has done. Let all who seek the Lord rejoice and proudly bear his name. He recalls his promises and leads his people forth in joy with shouts of thanksgiving. Alleluia. Alleluia.	The Body (Blood) of our Lord Jesus Christ keep you in everlasting life. **[Amen.]**
	After Communion, the Celebrant says
OR	Let us pray.
	Celebrant and People
Lord, now you let your servant go in peace; your word has been fulfilled. My own eyes have seen the salvation which you have prepared in the sight of every people; A light to reveal you to the nations and the glory of your people Israel. Glory to the Father, and to the Son, and to the Holy Spirit, as it was in the beginning, is now, and will be forever. Amen	**Eternal God, heavenly Father, you have graciously accepted us as living members of your Son our Savior Jesus Christ, and you have fed us with spiritual food in the Sacrament of his Body and Blood. Send us now into the world in peace, and grant us strength and courage to love and serve you with gladness and singleness of heart; through Jesus Christ our Lord. Amen.**

32) The administration of the sacrament is choreographed in a variety of ways in both churches. Architecture and furnishing, of course, have a significant impact on how things are done. Episcopalians have always insisted on the common cup, and the Book of Common Prayer commends the practice of having only one chalice on the altar at the time of the Consecration. The one cup signifies the oneness of the people of God, the unity of the church. The New Testament indicates that Jesus passed around one cup of wine. However, Episcopalians have not always insisted on one loaf of bread. Episcopalians use real wine for communion, but not necessarily real bread. Both Lutherans and Episcopalians often use wafers that bear little resemblance to anything that might be called bread. Most Episcopalians may be scandalized by the tiny, individual communion cups sometimes used by Lutherans. Conversely, some Lutherans nowadays would be loathe to receive from a common chalice, although that was once their own norm. Perhaps they need to know that the Episcopal Church permits intinction (the dipping of the bread into the wine) and allows a communicant to receive in one kind only. The common cup and the administration of wine to the communicants are inheritances of the Reformation (and of the primitive church) and are strong among Lutherans in some parts of the world. It should be noted that through the centuries there have been innumerable ways of administering this sacrament. The Greeks mix the wine and the bread and administer the mixed elements with a spoon. In the early medieval period in Western Europe the consecrated wine was sometimes drunk through a straw! We do not have the luxury of imagining that there is one and only one proper and orthodox way to administer communion.

40. One of these prayers is said.	*or the following*

We give you thanks almighty God, that you have refreshed us through the healing power of this gift of life; and we pray that in your mercy you would strengthen us, through this gift, in faith toward you and in fervent love toward one another; for the sake of Jesus Christ our Lord.

OR

Pour out upon us the spirit of your love, O Lord, and unite the wills of those whom you have fed with one heavenly food; through Jesus Christ our Lord.

OR

Almighty God, you gave your Son both as a sacrifice for sin and a model of the godly life. Enable us to receive him always with thanksgiving, and to conform our lives to his; through the same Jesus Christ our Lord.

Amen

Almighty and everliving God, we thank you for feeding us with the spiritual food of the most precious Body and Blood of your Son our Savior Jesus Christ; and for assuring us in these holy mysteries that we are living members of the Body of your Son and heirs of your eternal kingdom. And now, Father, send us out to do the work you have given us to do, to love and serve you as faithful witnesses of Christ our Lord. To him, to you, and to the Holy Spirit, be honor and glory, now and for ever. Amen.

33)

41. Silence for reflection.

42. The minister blesses the congregation.

Almighty God, Father, Son, and Holy Spirit, bless you now and forever.

OR

The Bishop when present, or the Priest, may bless the people.

The Deacon, or the Celebrant, dismisses them with these words

> Let us go forth in the name of Christ.

People **Thanks be to God.**

33) Both liturgies allow for a hymn or anthem before and after the postcommunion prayer. And both provide for a blessing to be pronounced by the ranking clergy person present. The Lutheran minister may use the Aaronic Blessing (Numbers 6:24-26). Both Lutherans and Episcopalians are heirs of the understanding of the eucharist as "a sending." The word *mass* is presumably derived from the Latin *missa*, a form of the verb that means "to send." (Medieval and Tridentine Latin masses ended with the idiomatic expression *Ite missa est*.) One meaning of the Greek verb *apostello*, from which we get "apostolic," is "to send out," and one sense in which the church is apostolic is that it is continually sending its people out on mission for the life of the world: sending them out as functional parts of the Body of Christ, to do God's will. We receive forgiveness and the spiritual nourishment of the sacrament and are immediately dispatched into the world to do the work of Christ, to labor for the advancement of his kingdom, and to engage in the ongoing struggle for the reconciliation of human beings with each other and with God. The postcommunion prayer, blessing, and dismissal follow quickly after the administration of the sacrament, and the service ends. Long standing custom in both traditions has the people depart with the singing of a hymn as the disciples did at the Last Supper (Matthew 26:30 and Mark 14:26). Any long or elaborate liturgy following communion is anticlimactic.

The Lord bless you and keep you.
The Lord make his face to shine on
you and be gracious to you.
The Lord look upon you with favor
and give you peace.

Amen

The minister may dismiss the congregation.

Go in peace. Serve the Lord.

Thanks be to God.

or this

Deacon Go in peace to love and
         serve the Lord.
People **Thanks be to God.**

or this

Deacon Let us go forth into the
         world, rejoicing in the power
         of the Spirit.
People **Thanks be to God.**

or this

Deacon Let us bless the Lord.
People **Thanks be to God.**

*From the Easter Vigil through the Day
of Pentecost "Alleluia, alleluia" may be
added to any of the dismissals.*

The People respond
Thanks be to God. Alleluia, alleluia

NOTE CONCERNING THE LIMA DOCUMENT (BEM)

A very significant milestone on the quest for unity among Christians was achieved at an international conference of theologians, scholars, and other church leaders held in Lima, Peru, in 1982. That milestone was the publication of the "Lima Document" entitled *Baptism, Eucharist, and Ministry*. It lists twenty-one "elements" that exist "in varying sequence and of diverse importance" in the eucharistic liturgies of all Christian bodies:

Hymns of praise
Act of repentance
Declaration of pardon
Proclamation of the Word of God
Confession of faith (creed)
Intercession for the whole church and for the world
Preparation of the bread and wine
Thanksgiving to the Father for the marvels of creation, redemption, and sanctification
The words of Christ's institution of the sacrament
The *anamnesis*, or memorial of the great acts of redemption, passion, death, resurrection, ascension, and Pentecost, which brought the church into being
The invocation of the Holy Spirit, *epiklesis*, on the community, and the elements of bread and wine
Consecration of the faithful to God
Reference to the communion of saints
Prayer for the return of the Lord and the definitive manifestation of his kingdom
The "Amen" of the whole community
The Lord's Prayer
A sign of reconciliation and peace

The breaking of the bread
Eating and drinking in communion with Christ and with
    each member of the church
Final act of praise
Blessing and sending

The Lutheran and Episcopal eucharistic liturgies contain all these "elements." This may be grounds enough for declaring them "sufficient" in the judgment of the church catholic.

THE BAPTISMAL LITURGY

—— ⑥ ——

Go therefore and make disciples of all people,
baptizing them in the name of the Father and of the Son
and of the Holy Spirit.

Matthew 28:19

AN OUTLINE

	LBW	BCP
	Lutheran Book of Worship	Book of Common Prayer
Presentation of Candidates	p. 121	p. 301
Renunciations and Act of Adherence	p. 123	p. 302
Baptismal Covenant (Profession of Faith)	p. 123	p. 304
Prayers for the Candidates	p. 122	p. 305
Thanksgiving Over the Water	p. 122	p. 306
The Baptism	p. 123	p. 307
Prayer for the Holy Spirit (Laying on of Hands)	p. 124	p. 308
Insignation (Sealing)	p. 124	p. 308
Welcome and Peace	p. 124	p. 308

Both Lutheran and Episcopal services contain the same fundamental prayers and action; however, the order in which they are performed may differ slightly. The Thanksgiving Over the Water, for example, comes before the Renunciations and Covenant in the Lutheran rite, but after them in the Episcopal rite.

Both Lutherans and Episcopalians regard Holy Baptism (with water and in the name of the Holy Trinity) as full initiation into the visible Body of Christ which is his church. Both view Holy Baptism as a gift from God, like birth and life itself, given to us who have no intrinsic merit of our own whereby we might deserve or desire it. Since baptism makes us members of Christ's church and gives us access to his apostolic fellowship, Word and Sacraments, it is clearly a means of grace and not just a sign.

[Baptisms normally take place as a part of the Sunday morning worship in the Lutheran Church. However, the LBW rubrics are not explicit about how the baptismal rite is integrated or attached to the regular liturgy.]

1)

[The order of the service is different in the two uses. Here, for purposes of comparison, we have edited the Episcopal use to conform to the order of the Lutheran use. For example: the Prayer over the Water in the Episcopal use comes after the baptismal vows, creed/covenant, and immediately before the baptism itself. Here we have moved it to the Lutheran place, earlier in the service.]

Holy Baptism

1. While a baptismal hymn is sung, the candidates, sponsors, and parents gather at the font.

2. The minister addresses the baptismal group and the congregation.

In Holy Baptism our gracious heavenly Father liberates us from sin and death by joining us to the death and resurrection of our Lord Jesus Christ. We are born children of a fallen humanity; in the waters of Baptism we are reborn children of God and inheritors of eternal life. By water and the Holy Spirit we are made members of the Church which is the body of Christ. As we live with him and with his people, we grow in faith, love, and obedience to the will of God.

Holy Baptism

(The same opening acclamations are used for a Baptism as for any communion service.)

The Celebrant continues

There is one Body and one Spirit;

People   **There is one hope in God's call to us;**

Celebrant One Lord, one Faith, one Baptism;

People   **One God and Father of all**

Celebrant The Lord be with you.

People   **And also with you.**

Celebrant Let us pray.

The Collect of the Day

People   **Amen.**

COMMENTARY

1) Both traditions discourage "private" baptisms and encourage the practice of performing baptisms on Sundays and on festivals that have special reference to baptism. Thomas Cranmer wrote the following for the first *Book of Common Prayer* (1549).

> It appeareth by ancient writers that the Sacrament of Baptism in the old time was not commonly ministered but at two times in the year, at Easter and Whitsuntide, at which times it was openly ministered in the presence of all the congregation: Which custom (now being grown out of use) although it cannot for many considerations be well restored again, yet it is thought good to follow the same as near as conveniently may be: Wherefore the people are to be admonished that it is most convenient that baptism should not be ministered but upon Sundays and other holy days when the most number of people come together [spelling modernized].

Baptism is initiation into the Christian family, the Body of Christ, and a representative assembly of the faithful should be gathered to welcome the newly baptized. *The Book of Common Prayer* 1979 specifically designates the Easter Vigil, the Day of Pentecost (Whitsunday), All Saints' Day (or the Sunday following), and the First Sunday after the Epiphany as particularly appropriate times for baptism. Today the norm in both Lutheran and Episcopal churches is for baptisms to be performed on Sunday within the eucharistic rite. However, both churches also allow for baptisms to be performed at other times and places and under other circumstances. Baptism is initiation into the universal church of Jesus Christ, not into a sect or merely into a local congregation. Both traditions hold Holy Baptism to be indelible and unrepeatable. Both traditions hold that a

*At the principal service on a Sunday or
other feast, the Collect and Lessons are
properly those of the Day. On other
occasions they are selected from "At
Baptism."*

The Lessons

The Sermon

3. *A sponsor for each candidate, in
turn, presents the candidate with these
or similar words:*

*Or the Sermon may be preached after
the Peace.*

**Presentation and Examination of
the Candidates**

I present ___name___ to receive the
Sacrament of Holy Baptism.

The Celebrant says
The Candidate(s) for Holy Baptism
will now be presented.

4. The minister addresses those candidates who are able to answer for
themselves:

Adults and Older Children

___name___, do you desire to be
baptized?

*The candidates who are able to answer
for themselves are presented individually
by their Sponsors, as follows*

Response I do.

2)

5. *The minister addresses the sponsors
and parents.*

Sponsor I present N. to receive the
Sacrament of Baptism.

6. *When only young children are baptized, the minister says:*
In Christian love you have presented
these children for Holy Baptism.
Your should, therefore, faithfully
bring them to the services of God'
house, and teach them the Lord's
Prayer, the Creed, and the Ten
Commandments. As they grow in
years, you should place in their
hands the Holy Scriptures and

*The Celebrant asks each candidate
when presented*
   Do you desire to be baptized?

Candidate I do.

Infants and Younger Children

*Then the candidates unable to answer
for themselves are presented individually
by their Parents and Godparents, as follows*

baptism should be performed or presided over by the person present who best represents the whole church or the person in whom the church has vested the most authority. If present, the bishop presides. If the bishop is not present but the pastor or rector is, then the pastor or rector presides and baptizes. If there are no clergy available, the lay person who is regarded as most representative of the church would do the baptism. Both churches make provision for emergency baptisms and conditional baptisms. Both provide opportunities for renewal of the baptismal covenant and for individuals to recall their own baptisms and renew the baptismal vows. Luther urged Christians to begin each morning with the recollection "I am a baptized person."

2) Both traditions continue to provide sponsors for the baptized. Sponsors of infants or small children are customarily called "godparents." The role of godparent has sometimes been sentimentalized or reduced to mere ceremonial. But both Lutherans and Episcopalians see very significant and positive roles for sponsors (godparents), regardless of the age of the baptismal candidate. The Lutheran rite is quite explicit and lists within the rite itself some specific duties of the sponsors. The Episcopal rite makes it appropriate for a sponsor to lead in the "Prayers for the Candidates," which outline boldly the characteristics of the Christian life into which it is anticipated the sponsor will lead the candidate, by the grace of God.

provide for their instruction in the Christian faith, that, living in the covenant of their Baptism and in communion with the Church, they may lead godly lives until the day of Jesus Christ.

Do you promise to fulfill these obligations?

Response I do.

7. *When older children and adults are baptized also, the minister says:*
In Christian love you have presented these people for Holy Baptism. You should therefore, faithfully care for them and help them in every way as God gives you opportunity, that they may bear witness to the faith we profess, and that, living in the covenant of their Baptism and in communion with the Church, they may lead godly lives until the day of Jesus Christ.

Do you promise to fulfill these obligations?

Response I do.

Stand

8. *When baptisms are celebrated within the Holy Communion, The Prayers may be said at this time, with special reference to those baptized.*

After each portion of the prayers:

Lord, in your mercy,

hear our prayer.

Parents and Godparents
I present N. to receive the Sacrament of Baptism.

When all have been presented the Celebrant asks the parents and godparents
Will you be responsible for seeing that the child you present is brought up in the Christian faith and life?

Parents and Godparents
I will, with God's help.

Celebrant
Will you be your prayers and witness help this child to grow into the full stature of Christ?

Parents and Godparents
I will, with God's help.

Prayers for the Candidates

The Celebrant then says to the congregation
Let us now pray for these persons who are to receive the Sacrament of new birth [and for those (this person) who have renewed their commitment to Christ.]

A person appointed leads the following petitions

Leader Deliver them, O Lord, from the way of sin and death.
People **Lord, hear our prayer.**

Leader Open their hearts to your grace and truth.
People **Lord, hear our prayer.**

3) A significant liturgical accomplishment of the Reformation of the sixteenth century was the reform of the baptismal rite and the restoration of more ancient and apostolic practices. The medieval church had added many innovations and embellished and elaborated the baptismal rite so extensively that the service was barely recognizable as baptism at all. For example, there was an *exsufflation* (a ceremonial breathing on the candidate), the *ephphatha* (a ceremony in which the ears and nose of the candidate were wetted with saliva), two anointings with oil, the giving of salt and a candle, and the vesting of the candidate in a baptismal gown. Both Luther and Cranmer were careful students of patristics, the study of the Fathers of the Church, and both sought to simplify and clarify the rite of Holy Baptism so that it looked and worked more like the ancient and apostolic rite. The early church had taken advantage of the rich symbolism of water to remind the faithful of the way water has been used in the story of salvation. In prayers said over the water, allusions were made to the waters of creation (Genesis 1:2, 6, 9 ff.; 2 Peter 3:5), the waters of death and chaos (Psalm 69:1-2 and Ezekiel 26:19), the waters of the great flood

Leader   Fill them with your holy and life-giving Spirit.
People   **Lord, hear our prayer.**

Leader   Keep them in the faith and communion of your holy Church.
People   **Lord, hear our prayer.**

Leader   Teach them to love others in the power of the Spirit.
People   **Lord, hear our prayer.**

Leader   Send them into the world in witness to your love.
People   **Lord, hear our prayer.**

Leader   Bring them to the fullness of your peace and glory.
People   **Lord, hear our prayer.**

The Celebrant says
Grant, O Lord, that all who are baptized into the death of Jesus Christ your Son may live in the power of his resurrection and look for him to come again in glory; who lives and reigns now and for ever. **Amen.**

3)   Thanksgiving over the Water

9. The minister begins the thanksgiving.

The Lord be with you.

And also with you.

Let us give thanks to the Lord our God.

It is right to give him thanks and praise.

The Celebrant blesses the water, first saying

The Lord be with you.
People   **And also with you.**

Celebrant Let us give thanks to the Lord our God.
People   **It is right to give him thanks and praise.**

3:5-6), the waters of the rivers of Paradise (Genesis 2:10 and Revelation 22:1-2), the water necessary to sustain life (Numbers 24:6; Psalm 107:35-38), the water from the rock on Sinai (Exodus 17:5-6; Psalm 105:41), the waters used for washing (Genesis 18:4; Exodus 29:4, 40:30-32; Deuteronomy 23:11; and John 13:5), the waters of the Red Sea in the Exodus (Exodus 15:1-10 and Deuteronomy 11:4), the waters of the Jordan in which Jesus was baptized (Matthew 3:13; Mark 1:9; and Deuteronomy 11:31-32). But in time these powerful theological images of salvation were replaced in the West by a more or less perfunctory blessing of the water to be used in baptism. Luther restored the ancient practice with his much loved "Flood Prayer" (*Sintflutgebet*). Cranmer was the first to translate this Prayer into English and he inserted it into the baptismal rite of the 1549 *Book of Common Prayer*:

Holy God, mighty Lord, gracious Father: We give you thanks, for in the beginning your Spirit moved over the waters and you created heaven and earth. By the gift of water you nourish and sustain us and all living things.

By the waters of the flood you condemned the wicked and saved those whom you had chosen, Noah and his family. You led Israel by the pillar of cloud and fire through the sea, out of slavery into the freedom of the promised land. In the waters of the Jordan your Son was baptized by John and anointed with the Spirit. By the baptism of his own death and resurrection your beloved Son has set us free from the bondage to sin and death, and has opened the way to the joy and freedom of everlasting life. He made water a sign of the kingdom and of cleansing and rebirth. In obedience to his command, we make disciples of all nations, baptizing them in the name of the Father, and of the Son, and of the Holy Spirit.

Pour out your Holy Spirit, so that those who are here baptized may be given new life. Wash away the sin of all those who are cleansed by this water and bring them forth as inheritors of your glorious kingdom.

To you be given praise and honor and worship through your Son, Jesus Christ our Lord, in the unity of the Holy Spirit, now and forever. **Amen.**

Celebrant
We thank you, Almighty God, for the gift of water. Over it the Holy Spirit moved in the beginning of creation Through it you led the children of Israe out of their bondage in Egypt into th Land of promise. In it your Son Jesu received the baptism of John and wa anointed by the Holy Spirit as the Messiah, the Christ, to lead us, throug his death and resurrection, from bondage of sin into everlasting life.

We thank you, Father, for the water of Baptism. In it we are buried with Christ in his death. By it we share i his resurrection. Through it we are reborn by the Holy Spirit. Therefore in joyful obedience to your Son, we bring into his fellowship those who come to him in faith, baptizing them in the Name of the Father, and of the Son, and of the Holy Spirit.

At the following words, the Celebrant touches the water

Now sanctify this water, we pray you, by the power of your Holy Spirit, that those who here are cleansed from sin and born again may continue for ever in the risen life of Jesus Christ, our Savior.

To him, to you, and to the Holy Spirit, be all honor and glory, now and for ever. **Amen.**

*Almighty and euerlastyng God, whiche of thy justice dydest
destroy by fluddes of water the whole worlde for synne, excepte
viii persons, whose of thy mercy (thesame tyme) thou didest
saue in the Arke: And when thou didest drowne in the read sea
wicked king Pharao with al his armie, yet (at thesame time)
thou didest leade thy people the chyldren of Israel safely through
the myddes therof: wherby thou didest fygure the washying of
thy holy Baptisme: And by the Baptisme of thy welbeloued
sonne Jesus Christe, thou dydest sanctifie the fludde Jordan,
and al other water to this misticall washing away of synne: We
beseeche thee (for thy infinite mercies) that thou wilt merciful-
ly looke vpon these children, and sanctifie them with thy holy
gost, that by this holesome lauer of regeneracioun, whatsoeuer
synne is in them, may be washed cleane away, that they being
deliuered from thy wrathe, may be receiued into tharke of
Christes churche, and so saued from peryshyng.*

10. The minister addresses the baptismal group and the congregation	*Then the Celebrant asks the following questions of the candidates who can speak for themselves, and of the parent and godparents who speak on behalf of the infants and younger children*
I ask you to profess your faith in Christ Jesus, reject sin, and confess the faith of the Church, the faith in which we baptize.	
4)	*Question* Do you renounce Satan and all the spiritual forces of wickedness that rebel against God?
Do you renounce all the forces of evil, the devil, and all his empty promises?	
	Answer I renounce them.
Response I do.	
	Question Do you renounce the evil powers of this world which corrupt and destroy the creatures of God?
	Answer I renounce them.
	Question Do you renounce all sinful desires that draw you from the love of God?
	Answer I renounce them.
	Question Do you turn to Jesus Christ and accept him as your Savior
	Answer I do.
	Question Do you put your whole trust in his grace and love?
	Answer I do.
	Question Do you promise to follow and obey him as your Lord?
	Answer I do.

Today Lutherans and Episcopalians (and Roman Catholics as well) use a greatly simplified rite and a "Thanksgiving Over the Water" that more closely resembles Luther's Flood Prayer than anything else. The use of a significant amount of water is encouraged, as is the practice of pouring the water into the font in full view of the congregation. The Episcopal rite prefers immersion, and the Lutheran rite calls for pouring water on the candidate three times. Thus, the clear and dramatic use of water is encouraged and the fundamental meaning of Holy Baptism is emphasized. Both traditions make conscious references to Paul's teaching in Romans 6:4 and Colossians 2:12 that we are buried with Christ in baptism in order that we may be risen with him and enter the life that lives beyond the tomb.

4) The threefold renunciations proclaimed in the Episcopal rite are of ancient origin. They have been seen as reflecting the threefold temptations and renunciations of Christ as recorded in Matthew 4:1-11. The renunciation of the "evil powers of this world which corrupt and destroy" parallels Jesus' temptation to turn stones into bread and his determination not to use his powers to pervert the natural order. The renunciation of "all sinful desires that draw you from the love of God" parallels Jesus' temptation to hurl himself off the pinnacle of the temple, testing God by doing a wild, foolish, suicidal act. And the renunciation of Satan, who promises earthly power to those who do his biding, was modeled by Jesus who said, "Away with you, Satan!" Satan, of course, is usually seen as a spiritual being, a fallen angel, the personification of evil, "the evil one." Lutherans today, taking their cue from the Second Vatican Council, use a simple one-sentence form for the renunciations.

LBW	BCP

	After all have been presented, the Celebran addresses the congregation, saying
	Will you who witness these vows d all in your power to support these persons in their life in Christ?
5)	
Do you believe in God the Father?	*People* We will.
I believe in God, the Father almighty, creator of heaven and earth.	*The Celebrant then says these or simila words*
	Let us join with those who are com mitting themselves to Christ and renew our own baptismal covenant.
Do you believe in Jesus Christ, the Son of God?	
I believe in Jesus Christ, his only Son, our Lord.	*Celebrant* Do you believe in God th Father?
He was conceived by the power of the Holy Spirit and born of the virgin Mary.	*People* **I believe in God, the Father almighty, creator of heaven and earth.**
He suffered under Pontius Pilate, was crucified, died, and was buried.	*Celebrant* Do you believe in Jesus Christ, the Son of God?
He descended into hell.*	
On the third day he rose again,	*People* **I believe in Jesus Christ, his only Son, our Lord.**
He ascended into heaven, and is seated at the right hand of the Father.	**He was conceived by the power of the Holy Spiri and born of the Virgin Mary.**
He will come again to judge the living and the dead.	**He suffered under Pontiu Pilate, was crucified, died, and was buried.**
	He descended to the dead
Do you believe in God the Holy Spirit?	**On the third day he rose again.**
I believe in the Holy Spirit, the holy catholic Church, the communion of saints, the forgiveness of sins, the resurrection of the body, and the life everlasting. Amen	**He ascended into heaven and is seated at the right hand of the Father**
	He will come again to judge the living and the dead.
Or, He descended to the dead	

5) The Apostles' Creed was the early baptismal creed in Rome. In the Western church it has become the standard form or symbol for a personal testimony of faith. (It has never been used in Eastern Orthodoxy.) Episcopalians add five promises and call the resultant package "The Baptismal Covenant." Each of the five promises have significant biblical references, but special note should be made of the first. This is drawn directly from the Revised Standard Version's translation of Acts 2:42: "They devoted themselves to the apostles' teaching and fellowship, to the breaking of bread and the prayers." The "apostles' teaching" may be read as a reference to the apostolic faith that is expressed in the creeds. The "apostles' fellowship" is seen by Episcopalians as a reference to the continuing apostolic community, represented by the apostolic episcopacy, that is the bishops. The "breaking of bread" is certainly a reference to Holy Communion and "the prayers" refers to the common liturgical prayers of the Christian community.

Celebrant Do you believe in God
           the Holy Spirit?

People   **I believe in the Holy Spirit,
           the holy catholic Church,
           the communion of saints,
           the forgiveness of sins,
           the resurrection of the body,
           and the life everlasting.**

6)

11. The minister baptizes each candidate.

Celebrant Will you continue in the
           apostles' teaching and
           fellowship, in the breaking
           of bread, and in the prayers?

___name___, I baptize you in the
name of the Father,
*The minister pours water on the candi-
date's head.*

People   **I will, with God's help.**

and of the Son,
*The minister pours water on the candi-
date's head a second time.*

Celebrant Will you persevere in
           resisting evil, and, when-
           ever you fall into sin, repent
           and return to the Lord?

and the Holy Spirit. Amen
*The minister pours water on the candi-
date's head a third time.*

People   **I will, with God's help.**

Celebrant Will you proclaim by word
           and example the Good
           News of God in Christ?

OR

People   **I will, with God's help.**

___name___ is baptized in the name
of the Father,
*The minister pours water on the candi-
date's head.*

Celebrant Will you seek and serve
           Christ in all persons, loving
           your neighbor as yourself?

People   **I will, with God's help.**

and of the Son,
*The minister pours water on the candi-
date's head a second time.*

Celebrant Will you strive for justice
           and peace among all people,
           and respect the dignity of
           every human being?

and of the Holy Spirit. Amen
*The minister pours water on the candi-
date's head a third time.*

People   **I will, with God's help.**

6) In Lutheran liturgy baptism is performed by pouring. The Episcopal rite has always shared with the Eastern churches a preference for immersion, but it permits pouring. In fact, pouring is the usual mode in both traditions. Neither permit sprinkling. Of course, the quantity of water does not affect the validity of the sacrament. It does affect the significance of the rite. Immersion symbolizes the candidate's going down into the dark waters of perdition and being raised up by God through the instrument of his holy church. It provides a dramatic visual aid, illustrative of the waters of chaos into which our lives are inevitably plunged and out of which God brings new life. Some are reminded of the gush of the uterine waters that accompany physical birth, and this gives an image of the regeneration (new birth into a new family) that actually takes place in Holy Baptism. Immersion provides the faithful with an image of conversion from the way of death to the way of eternal life, an image that we hope will be reflected in the life of the baptized, moving from sin and darkness into the life of grace. Pouring symbolizes a quieter dimension of the life of the baptized, but also an essential one to the washing away of sin. Sprinkling could hardly be seen as anything but trivial, or worse, magic. The church catholic has insisted on baptism in the name of the Holy Trinity since at least the fourth century. Baptism with water in the name of the Father, Son, and Holy Spirit is recognized the world over as valid and unrepeatable by the Lutheran, Anglican, Roman, Reformed, Methodist, and Eastern churches, regardless of who performs the rite. The *Lutheran Book of Worship* specifically prescribes triple pouring. *The Book of Common Prayer* is not so specific, but the same practice prevails in most churches of each denomination.

12. A psalm or hymn may be sung as the minister and the baptismal group go before the altar.

The Lord be with you.

And also with you.

Each candidate is presented by name to the Celebrant, or to an assisting priest or deacon, who then immerses, or pours water upon, the candidate, saying

N. , I baptize you in the Name of the Father, and of the Son, and of the Holy Spirit. **Amen.**

7)

13. Those who have been baptized kneel. Sponsors or parents holding young children stand. The minister lays both hands on the head of each of the baptized and prays for the Holy Spirit.

When this action has been completed for all candidates, the Bishop or Priest, at a place in full sight of the congregation, prays over them, saying

God, the Father of our Lord Jesus Christ, we give you thanks for freeing your sons and daughters from the power of sin and for raising them up to a new life through this holy sacrament. Pour you Holy Spirit upon ___name___: the spirit of wisdom and understanding, the spirit of counsel and might, the spirit of knowledge and the fear of the Lord, the spirit of joy in your presence. **Amen.**

Let us pray.
Heavenly Father, we thank you that by water and the Holy Spirit you have bestowed upon these your servants the forgiveness of sin, and have raised them to the new life of grace. Sustain them, O Lord, in your Holy Spirit. Give them an inquiring and discerning heart, the courage to will and to persevere, a spirit to know and to love you, and the gift of joy and wonder in all your works. **Amen.**

14. The minister marks the sign of the cross on the forehead of each of the baptized. Oil prepared for this purpose may be used. As the sign of the cross is made, the minister says:

Then the Bishop or Priest places a hand on the person's head, marking on the forehead the sign of the cross (using Chrism if desired) and saying to each one

___name___, child of God, you have been sealed by the Holy Spirit and marked with the cross of Christ forever.

N., you are sealed by the Holy Spirit in Baptism and marked as Christ's own for ever. **Amen.**

The sponsor or the baptized responds: "Amen."

7) Both traditions follow the baptism with a prayer for the Holy Spirit and with the Insignation or Sealing. The sign of the cross is made on the forehead of the candidate. Actually, in the early church this may have been the *chi* (the Greek initial of the Christ). It is alluded to in the Revelation to St. John 7:3 and in Ephesians 4:30: "Do not grieve the Holy Spirit of God, with which you were marked with a seal for the day of redemption." This is the anointing from which the very name "Christian" is derived; that is, from the Greek *christos*, an anointed one. A sweet-smelling oil, customarily made from olive oil, balsam, and cinnamon, that has been consecrated (blessed and set aside) for this purpose is normally used in the sealing. The Old Testament priests were anointed with oil, and this unction is a reminder that we are a priestly people. Baptized persons are expected to function as the priests of the Jewish Temple did, interceding and offering sacrifices for the salvation of all. Both Lutheran and Episcopal rites make explicit mention of this, and each has the laity make the point. Before the service ends, as a part of the welcoming of the newly baptized, the Lutheran use will have a representative of the congregation refer to "the priesthood we all share in Christ Jesus" and the Episcopal use will have the entire congregation invite the newly baptized to "share with us in his eternal priesthood."

15. After all have received the sign of the cross, they stand.

8)

16. A lighted candle may be given to each of the baptized (to the sponsor of a young child) by a representative of the congregation who says:

Let your light so shine before others that they may see your good works and glorify your Father in heaven.

Stand

9)

18. The ministers and the baptismal group turn toward the congregation; a representative of the congregation says:

Through Baptism God has made these new sisters and brothers members of the priesthood we share in Christ Jesus, that we may proclaim the praise of God and bear his creative and redeeming Word to all the world.

10)

We welcome you into the Lord's family. We receive you as fellow members of the body of Christ, children of the same heavenly Father, and workers with us in the kingdom of God.

19. The ministers may exchange the peace with the baptized, with their sponsors and parents, and with the congregation:

Peace be with you. Peace be with you.

20. All return to their places.

21. The service continues with the Offering.

[On page 313 of the *Book of Common Prayer* there is the following rubric: *After the Baptism, a candle (which may be lighted from the Paschal Candle) may be given to each of the newly baptized or to a godparent.*]

When all have been baptized, the Celebrant says

Let us welcome the newly baptized.

Celebrant and People

We receive you into the household of God. Confess the faith of Christ crucified, proclaim his resurrection, and share with us in his eternal priesthood.

If Confirmation, Reception, or Reaffirmation of Baptismal Vows is not to follow, the Peace is now exchanged.

Celebrant The peace of the Lord be always with you.
People **And also with you.**

The service continues with the Prayers of the People or the Offertory of the Eucharist, at which the Bishop, when present, should be the principal Celebrant.

8) Both rites make provision for the presentation of a lighted baptismal candle to the newly baptized. This custom is widely practiced in both churches, although it is optional. If a paschal candle is used, then the baptismal candle is lighted from it; otherwise it is lighted from one of the altar candles. The tradition is for the baptized person to light this candle and remember in prayer and thanksgiving the gift of Holy Baptism each year on the anniversary of the event.

9) Neither liturgy makes mention of the traditional white gown (*alba*) which is associated with Holy Baptism. In ancient times people were baptized in the nude, or nearly nude. (And so they are to this day in some of the Eastern churches.) After the baptism itself the candidate was dried and vested in a white robe (see Revelation 3:4-5 6:11, and 7:9). The white "thing" (*alba*), or alb, is the uniform of the baptized. In Northern Europe to baptize an infant, or an adult, in the nude in winter would be a dangerous thing to do. The churches were not often heated. The custom in the Western church came to be for the child or adult to come to baptism already vested or dressed in white. In recent times there has been a move to recover the more ancient practice, that of vesting the candidate after baptism. This, of course, is permissible in both the Lutheran and Episcopal traditions. The white gown represents the purity of Christ, which the baptized person "puts on."

10) Both liturgies conclude with a welcome or reception of the newly baptized and with the Peace. The "Peace" is the equivalent of the New Testament "kiss of peace" and the "right hand of fellowship."

SOME NOTES CONCERNING CEREMONIAL AND SETTING

In the early days of the church Christians stood for prayer and acts of praise, following the customs of their Jewish and Greek antecedents. It was customary to raise the open palms of ones' hands towards heaven in what came to be called the oranti (Latin, praying) position. Courtesy, then as now, demanded that one stand when addressing a superior or when in the presence of one who is held in honor or esteem. To sit, slouched in ones' chair, when speaking to a parent, a teacher, a commander, or an employer, would have been highly disrespectful. So, the faithful would not casually address the Deity while lounging about or seated.

In medieval Western Europe the custom of standing for prayer was modified. In feudal society the more flamboyant gesture of kneeling before ones' superiors came into vogue and was adopted by the faithful in church. Kneeling had, in ancient times, been regarded as a most extravagant gesture of humility and penance. In fact, the Council of Nicaea had forbidden Christians to use this gesture during the fifty days of Easter, it was so contrary to the spirit of joy and affirmation that should accompany the celebration of the Resurrection. But, in the middle ages it became a standard posture for prayer in Western Europe. The sixteenth century Reformers encouraged the faithful to return to the more ancient practice of standing for prayer and praise and kneeling only as an act of contrition. Most Lutheran and Episcopal churches conform to this standard today. The Vatican II Council of the Roman Catholic Church adopted the same standard in the twentieth century.

A dimension of Evangelical Catholic worship that almost defies description is the use of vestments, paraments, and other accouterments. An important characteristic that Lutherans and

Episcopalians share is that neither, in the days of the sixteenth century Reformation, chose to discard entirely the vestments, decorative art, and ceremonies of the medieval church. Of course, they did discard some practices which they regarded as corrupt, heterodox, or both. In some times and places, churches of each communion have adopted the clerical costuming popularized by the Calvinists: the black preaching gown with Geneva bands or a ruff. However, in each denomination the more ancient churchly vestments have prevailed. The alb, the white floor-length vestment, which is in fact the baptismal garment, is virtually universal. It is worn by officiating clergy, servers, and, sometimes, choir members. The surplice and cotta are variations of the alb, the former being fuller and the latter shorter. In most instances the priest or pastor wears a stole. This long, scarf-like item is customarily in the color of the season or of the particular occasion: white for Easter and Christmas, red for Pentecost, and so forth. The stole is actually of pre-Christian Roman origin, but since the sixteenth century it has been prescribed to be worn by all Catholic clergy in priestly (presbyteral or episcopal) orders. When officiating at non sacramental services, such as Morning or Evening Prayer or the Burial Office, Episcopal clergy often wear "choir habit" (as do some Lutherans as well). This consists of the long black medieval clerical undergarment called a cassock, over which is worn a long, flowing white surplice and a black tippet (preaching scarf). An academic hood is sometimes worn with this attire. The chasuble, the priest's mass vestment in the medieval Latin church, is often worn by Episcopal priests when celebrating the Holy Eucharist. It is less frequently used in Lutheran churches. A chasuble is a one-piece (poncho like) sleeveless vestment, oval shaped with a hole in the center for the head, that is draped over the shoulders and hangs down to below the knees. Like the stole, it is usually of the color appropriate to the season or occasion.

Both Lutherans and Episcopalians have kept the traditional

Christian year, with local or national variation from time to time and place to place. Both observe the four weeks of Advent that lead up to the Twelve Days of Christmas: the annual celebration of the Incarnation of God, called the Nativity of the Lord Jesus Christ. Both churches celebrate the Epiphany, recalling especially the visit of the Wise Men (Three Kings), the Baptism of the Lord, and the first miracle at Cana of Galilee. For both, the weeks after Epiphany climax with the Sunday of the Transfiguration. Then come the solemn forty days of Lent that begin with Ash Wednesday. The last week of the Lenten fast begins with Passion Sunday (commonly called Palm Sunday) and culminates in the sacred Triduum: Maundy Thursday, Good Friday, and Easter. The focus by then has shifted to the Atonement and the celebration of the victory of Jesus Christ over evil and death. Easter Day, the Feast of the Resurrection of the Lord, is the apogee of the Christian year. It commences the Great Fifty Days of Eastertide. The celebration of the Ascension of Jesus comes near the end of the Great Fifty Days, and the season ends with Pentecost (the fiftieth day), the celebration of the empowering of the church by the Holy Spirit. In both traditions, the first Sunday after Pentecost is called Trinity Sunday. Then we enter the "long green season" of the weeks after Pentecost. The vestments and paraments are green at this time, a period that Roman Catholics call Ordinary Time.

All of the seasons and times mentioned here are celebrated by Lutherans and Episcopalians in almost exactly the same way and certainly with the same essential theological and pastoral messages. Even the colors of the vestments and paraments are the same, unless a particular church is following a variant color schedule, which is quite permissible in both denominations. The Episcopal Church observes seven Principal Feasts, which take precedence over all other celebrations, even Sundays. These seven are Easter Day, Ascension Day, the Day of Pentecost, Trinity Sunday, All Saints' Day, Christmas Day, and the Epiphany. Lutherans observe the same Principal Festivals with the exception of All Saints' Day, which is observed as Reformation Day (or Reformation Sunday). It was on the feast of All Saints that Martin Luther posted his famous Ninety-five Theses on the door of the Castle Church in Wittenberg. Both churches observe Ash Wednesday and Good Friday as special days of prayer and fasting. The Episcopal Church has traditionally made more of "red letter" saints' days than have Lutherans, especially the Marian feasts: the Presentation (February 2), the Annunciation (March 25), the Visitation (May 31), and Saint Mary the Virgin Mother of the Lord (August 15).

Church architecture and furniture tell us much about the translation and continuation of Lutheran (Evangelical) and Episcopal (Anglican) liturgical traditions in America. The English Colonies provided British and European Protestants with great opportunities to build new churches. The old world had an abundance of splendid church buildings, but the new world had none until the colonists built them. Those in the Puritan and radical camps (Congregationalists, Presbyterians, Baptists, and Quakers) built "meeting houses" that were different from any churches the world had ever seen. They were stark and plain and unadorned by even so much as a simple cross. Except for the Quaker structures, they were pulpit centered to suit their sermon centered liturgies. The Anglicans also experimented with innovative designs for houses of worship. Some "modern," seventeenth century, Anglican churches in America featured a prayer desk, lectern, pulpit combination on the liturgical south wall, a holy table for communion on the east wall, and a baptismal font on the west wall. Parishioners stood, sat, and knelt in family box pews in the center, from which they could turn easily in any direction as the action and focus of the service moved. This pattern of architecture and furniture dramatically emphasized the proclamation of the Word and the two chief sacraments, Holy Baptism and Holy Communion.

On the whole, looking back over nearly four hundred years of Episcopal and Lutheran church building in America, it is remarkable how consistent the pattern has been. Our churches have been altar centered, in sharp contrast to the Puritan meeting houses. Our churches have been altar centered even when our liturgical practices have veered away from the eucharistic norm. In the days of the Reformation both Luther and Cranmer advocated that the eucharist should continue to be the principal service on the Lord's Day. However, some Lutherans, influenced no doubt by their Calvinist/Reformed neighbors, observed only the antecommunion (pro-anaphora/liturgy of the word) on most Sundays. Some Episcopalians, touched by the same influences, did exactly the same thing. And some gathered on Sunday morning just for Morning Prayer and Sermon. But even then the architecture and furniture betrayed the fact that we both were still, heart and soul, eucharistic communities.

CONCLUSIONS:
SO NOW WHAT?

Evangelical Catholic liturgy aims at proclaiming and presenting Jesus Christ, God Incarnate. In the liturgy we stand in awe and wonder at God who is transcendent. We celebrate with joy and thanksgiving God who is immanent and loving. The one, true, and living God passes through our senses and emotions and penetrates where our limited reasoning powers cannot take us. The liturgy, Word and Sacrament, is the life source of the church. It is a gift of God. If we are going to evaluate and judge the way the liturgy is done in one place or another, and God gives most of us the temerity to do so, it should be on the basis of how effectively Jesus Christ is communicated, how genuinely his presence is known and responded to by the people and how keenly the worshipers are aware of the mystery of the Incarnation.

There is no substitute for being there. One must be present and participate in a liturgy in order to understand and appreciate it. Reading a liturgy, or reading about a liturgy, is rather like reading orchestral sheet music. Only an astute professional could get much out of reading the score of Beethoven's Ninth if he had never heard it. In order for Episcopalians and Lutherans to benefit from each other's liturgical genius, each must find time and opportunity to experience the other's liturgy. In order for Presbyterians, Baptists, Eastern Orthodox, or Roman Catholics to find enrichment and renewal in Evangelical Catholic worship, they will simply have to attend and participate. Nor can Buddhists or Muslims, agnostics or atheists, hope to understand and appreciate the essential nature of Christianity unless they have at least attended some Christian liturgies.

Present relationships between the Episcopal and Lutheran judicatories in America include "interim eucharist sharing." This means that Lutherans can attend and participate fully in Episcopal worship and vice versa. As yet it appears that only a relatively small number of individuals and parishes have found ways to take advantage of this opportunity to share in Christ. When this sharing has happened, it has usually occurred as part of a special event or under unusual circumstances: at a joint vacation Bible school, at a conference or retreat, or in a seminary or college setting. However, more and more Episcopal and Lutheran churches that share the same neighborhood turf are finding opportunities to share liturgically. It is hoped that this little book will encourage further participation.

There is an important caveat. Many people think that their local parish is typical of their denomination. This may or may not be so. You may attend a dozen parishes and never stumble on one that is truly "typical." One of the advantages of the kind of structured liturgy of each of these communions is that it allows for a great deal of local variation and choice. So the style and ethos of an Anglo-Catholic "high church" service in Wisconsin may not be the same at all as that of a staunchly Protestant "low church" service in Virginia. The service in a Lutheran congregation of Swedish extraction may look and feel quite different from that of a German congregation. Not all Lutherans are Midwestern farmers, and not all Episcopalians are Eastern plutocrats. Your author knows of at least two Episcopal churches in the rural South in which virtually every member is on welfare, and one would have to go far to find a wealthier, more sophisticated and more "Eastern Establishment" congregation than that of St. Peter's Lutheran in Manhattan, New York City. Each denomination is a fascinating patchwork quilt. It is the Holy Spirit and the liturgy of Word and Sacrament that holds each communion together.

In this modest volume we have looked only at Evangelical Catholic liturgies for Holy Baptism and Holy Communion. Granted, these are the chief sacraments, regarded as "generally necessary for salvation" by each party. But thoughtful and caring Christians of both denominations will want to consider and compare the Lutheran and Episcopal expression of the Great Litany, the Christian Calendar and Biblical Lectionary (propers and pericopes), the Daily Offices, and the rites for Confirmation, Holy Matrimony, Ordination, Anointing of the Sick, and Burial of the Dead. For such further study there are four books that are simply essential:

The Lutheran Book of Worship, 1978
Manual on the Liturgy, by Philip H. Pfatteicher and Carlos R. Messerli, Augsburg, Minneapolis, 1979
The Book of Common Prayer, 1979
Commentary on the American Prayer Book, by Marion J. Hatchett, Seabury, New York, 1980

In this cursory look at the two liturgies, we have considered only the contemporary English forms. There are Spanish, French, and Native American versions of the *Book of Common Prayer* and, similarly versions of the *Lutheran Book of Worship* in various languages. There are many historical recensions, and to this day some Episcopalians and some Lutherans prefer to worship in archaic varieties of English or other languages, which is tolerated to a limited extent by each group.

As a young priest fresh from seminary, I went to visit an old, old Christian who lay on his deathbed. He was weak but coherent. We visited briefly, and I placed my hand in his and offered the kind of elegant, sensitive, and theologically sound prayer that only a recent seminary graduate could utter. I knew he was touched, and I even suspected that God might have been as well. After the "Amen" the old man said, "That was a wonderful prayer. Thank you." Then with trembling hand he reached over and picked up the tattered *Prayer Book* that lay on the bedside table. He placed it in my hand and said, "Now, let's pray the prayer of the church." And so we did. This is what I would want to say to my Lutheran and Episcopal sisters and brothers today: Now, let's pray the prayer of the church.